THE NEW COLLEGEVILLE BIBLE COMMENTARY

AMOS
HOSEA
MICAH
NAHUM
ZEPHANIAH
HABAKKUK

Carol J. Dempsey, OP

SERIES EDITOR

Daniel Durken, O.S.B.

Collegeville, Minnesota

www.litpress.org

Nihil Obstat: Reverend Robert Harren, *Censor deputatus*.
Imprimatur: ✠ Most Reverend John F. Kinney, J.C.D., D.D., Bishop of St. Cloud, Minnesota, April 15, 2013.

Design by Ann Blattner.

Cover illustration: *Demands of Social Justice* by Suzanne Moore. © 2007 *The Saint John's Bible*, Saint John's University, Collegeville, Minnesota USA. Used by permission. Scripture quotations are from the New Revised Standard Version of the Bible, Catholic Edition, copyright 1989, 1993 National Council of the Churches of Christ in the United States of America. Used by permission. All rights reserved.

Photos: pages 8, 38, 76, 104, and 130, Sanctuary of Bom Jesus of Matosinhos at Congonhas, Minas Gerais, Brazil; page 116, icon of Zephaniah, Wikimedia Commons.

Maps created by Robert Cronan of Lucidity Information Design, LLC.

1   2   3   4   5   6   7   8   9

Library of Congress Cataloging-in-Publication Data

Dempsey, Carol J.
    Amos, Hosea, Micah, Nahum, Zephaniah, Habakkuk / Carol J. Dempsey, OP
        pages cm. — (New Collegeville Bible Commentary. Old Testament ;
    Volume 15)
    Includes index.
    ISBN 978-0-8146-2849-2 (alk. paper)
    1. Bible. O.T. Minor Prophets—Commentaries.   I. Title.
    BS1560.D46   2013
    224'.907—dc23   2013008344

CONTENTS

ABBREVIATIONS

Books of the Bible

Acts—Acts of the Apostles
Amos—Amos
Bar—Baruch
1 Chr—1 Chronicles
2 Chr—2 Chronicles
Col—Colossians
1 Cor—1 Corinthians
2 Cor—2 Corinthians
Dan—Daniel
Deut—Deuteronomy
Eccl (or Qoh)—Ecclesiastes
Eph—Ephesians
Esth—Esther
Exod—Exodus
Ezek—Ezekiel
Ezra—Ezra
Gal—Galatians
Gen—Genesis
Hab—Habakkuk
Hag—Haggai
Heb—Hebrews
Hos—Hosea
Isa—Isaiah
Jas—James
Jdt—Judith
Jer—Jeremiah
Job—Job
Joel—Joel
John—John
1 John—1 John
2 John—2 John
3 John—3 John
Jonah—Jonah
Josh—Joshua
Jude—Jude
Judg—Judges
1 Kgs—1 Kings

2 Kgs—2 Kings
Lam—Lamentations
Lev—Leviticus
Luke—Luke
1 Macc—1 Maccabees
2 Macc—2 Maccabees
Mal—Malachi
Mark—Mark
Matt—Matthew
Mic—Micah
Nah—Nahum
Neh—Nehemiah
Num—Numbers
Obad—Obadiah
1 Pet—1 Peter
2 Pet—2 Peter
Phil—Philippians
Phlm—Philemon
Prov—Proverbs
Ps(s)—Psalms
Rev—Revelation
Rom—Romans
Ruth—Ruth
1 Sam—1 Samuel
2 Sam—2 Samuel
Sir—Sirach
Song—Song of Songs
1 Thess—1 Thessalonians
2 Thess—2 Thessalonians
1 Tim—1 Timothy
2 Tim—2 Timothy
Titus—Titus
Tob—Tobit
Wis—Wisdom
Zech—Zechariah
Zeph—Zephaniah

Amos

The book of Amos, resplendent with a variety of rhetorical forms expressive of a polished, impassioned, dynamic, and didactic style, captures the imaginations of readers with its straightforward, "in-your-face" message. The prophet wastes no time in drawing attention to the horrific injustices of his day (1:2–5:3; 5:7, 10-13; 5:16–9:10). Such a vision, however, is not without words of encouragement (5:4-9, 14-15) and a vision of future restoration (9:11-15), one that speaks of hope and not despair, life and not death. Amos, the book's prophet, addresses his message to a host of mighty nations guilty of horrendous deeds and horrific injustices (1:3–2:16); to Judah (2:4-5) and Israel (2:6–3:15) for their transgressions; to those living in Samaria who are guilty of oppression and abuse (4:1-3); and to all other Israelites who have failed to keep covenant and live according to God's ways (5:7–6:14). The lot of wayward Israel will be pain, suffering, and devastation at the hand of Israel's God, all of which they will be warned about by the prophet Amos, who will be shown a series of divine visions that outline the impending disasters (7:1–9:10). Despite all of the foreboding news for Israel, the people will not be left without a glimmer of hope. The book of Amos closes on a positive note: in days to come, God will restore the people of Israel (7:11-15). Like so many of the prophets of biblical times, Amos heralds a God who metes out punitive justice for the sake of re-establishing right relationship and restoring the people to their land and to covenant fidelity.

The historical and social world of Amos

Whether or not Amos is an actual historical person has been debated among some scholars, but some evidence does exist that suggests he was someone who came from Judah and traveled to Israel, where he conducted his prophetic activity during the first half of the eighth century B.C. Israel's king at the time was Jeroboam II (786–746 B.C.). Judah's king was Uzziah (783–742 B.C.). Jeroboam II was the last king in the northern kingdom's longest dynasty known as the Jehu dynasty. During Jeroboam II's reign,

Egypt, Assyria, and Babylon were not yet formidable nations or threats to Israel. The king had successfully subdued the Arameans, who were Israel's most powerful enemy (2 Kgs 14:25-28). Furthermore, no strife between Israel and Judah existed at this time. For Israel, the early part of the eighth century B.C. was a time of prosperity that brought with it, unfortunately, the exploitation of the poor and defenseless by the wealthy and the powerful. With a new economic order came excessive wealth for some Israelites, which, in turn, led to a leisured upper class, many of whom became involved in decadent lifestyles (2:8; 4:1; 6:1-6). Judicial corruption also took root (5:7-12) along with religious hypocrisy. Into this world of affluence, exploitation, and profit stepped Amos, who has long been called God's prophet of social justice.

The literary dimensions of the book of Amos

The book of Amos is a rich literary text that contains a wide variety of forms, such as admonitions (e.g., 5:6, 14-15), laments (e.g., 5:1-17), and narratives (e.g., 7:10-17). The text also features a variety of literary techniques that include the repetition of stock phrases, such as graded numerical sayings (e.g., 1:3, 6, 9, 11, 13; 2:1, 4, 6), rhetorical questions (e.g., 2:11; 3:3-6, 8; 5:18, 25; 6:2; 8:8; 9:7), similes (e.g., 2:13; 5:24; 6:5; 8:8; 9:5, 7), metaphors (e.g., 4:1; 5:2), antitheses (e.g., 5:4-5), and quotations (e.g., 7:1-17). These forms and devices attest to the literary artistry of the text and support its appeal to the ethical consciousness and theological imagination of its readers.

As a literary work, the text can be subdivided into six main literary units and their respective subdivisions:

I. Superscription and introduction (1:1-2)
II. Proclamations concerning the nations (1:3–2:16)
   Concerning Aram/Damascus (1:3-5)
   Concerning Philistia (1:6-8)
   Concerning Tyre (1:9-10)
   Concerning Edom (1:11-12)
   Concerning Ammon (1:13-15)
   Concerning Moab (2:1-3)
   Concerning Judah (2:4-5)
   Concerning Israel (2:6-16)
III. Three words to Israel (3:1–5:6, 8-9)
   First word (3:1-15)
   Second word (4:1-13)
   Third word (5:1-6, 8-9)

The prophet Amos, sculpted by Aleijadinho, in front of the church of the Sanctuary of Bom Jesus of Matosinhos at Congonhas, Minas Gerais, Brazil.

IV. Three woes (5:7, 10-17; 5:18-27; 6:1-14)

First woe (5:7, 10-17)

Second woe (5:18-27)

Third woe (6:1-14)

V. Five visions; two judgment speeches (7:1–9:10)

First vision: locust (7:1-3)

Second vision: fire (7:4-6)

Third vision: the plummet (7:7-9)

First judgment speech concerning Amaziah, his family, and Israel (7:10-17)

Fourth vision: summer fruit (8:1-3)

Second judgment speech concerning Israel's unjust inhabitants (8:4-14)

Fifth vision: God (9:1-10)

VI. Epilogue (9:11-15)

Finally, in order to lend authority and credence to the prophet's words, the poet routinely uses the phrase "Thus says the LORD," which is a traditional prophetic messenger formula added secondarily to the poems themselves. Thus, the poetry of the book of Amos with its defined climactic patterns (for three transgressions . . . and for four) complemented by the text's rich metaphorical language and use of literary devices, is a literary tapestry whose ethical message is both disturbing and hopeful.

The theological dimensions of the book of Amos

Without a doubt, the book of Amos is primarily concerned with social justice. For Amos, this was the God of the poor, the needy, and the oppressed. This God was also "the God of hosts" (3:13)—the commander-in-chief of all that exists in the heavenly court and on earth. This God is sovereign over all territories and peoples (1:3–2:16), over individuals such as Amaziah and his family (7:10-17), and even over Amos himself, insofar as he was called to be a prophet by God quite unexpectedly (7:14-15). This God has the power to depose kings (7:9) and even the people whom this God loves so dearly (8:1-3). This emphasis on sovereignty reflects the poet's agenda to push monotheism in a culture and world where polytheism prevailed even in Judah and in Israel.

From a hermeneutical perspective, the portrait of God as presented in the book of Amos reflects the culture of the day, and, like the other biblical Prophetic Books, the poet's description is anthropomorphic, anthropocentric, and androcentric. Amos's portrayal of God is disturbing, but from a metaphorical perspective, the description is effective in a time when political, social, and religious leaders were amassing more and more power and wealth at the expense of the poor. Israel's larger-than-life God who minces no words and holds back no punitive justice is far more powerful than the greatest of all leaders on earth. Eventually the inevitable will strike Israel, Judah, and the nations—they will suffer defeat at the hands of enemy forces, which the prophet attributes to God. The people of Amos's day live under divine threat, and history bears out that they do not change their ways even when they are being threatened. Israel also lives under promise (9:11-15). Permanent destruction and devastation is not to be Israel and the nations' everlasting lot. Re-creation and restoration is the final word, the final deed, and ultimately the final divine intention of a God whose transformative power continues to bring beauty and life out of ash heaps and ruins.

Amos

I. Editorial Introduction

1 ¹The words of Amos, who was one of the sheepbreeders from Tekoa, which he received in a vision concerning Israel in the days of Uzziah, king of Judah, and in the days of Jeroboam, son of Joash, king of Israel, two years before the earthquake. ²He said:

> The LORD roars from Zion,
> and raises his voice from
> Jerusalem;

The pastures of the shepherds
languish,
and the summit of Carmel
withers.

II. Oracles against the Nations

Aram

³Thus says the LORD:

> For three crimes of Damascus,
> and now four—
> I will not take it back—

SUPERSCRIPTION AND INTRODUCTION

Amos 1:1-2

The book of Amos opens with a superscription that identifies Amos and his historical times. Both Uzziah and Jeroboam ruled during the eighth century B.C. Both Amos (1:1) and Zechariah (14:5) refer to a literal earthquake during the reign of Uzziah, king of Judah. Neither Amos nor Zechariah gives any further identification of detail about the earthquake except to say that it had happened. This occurrence must have been destructive and familiar to Amos's and Zechariah's readers. The anthropomorphic description of God raising the divine voice from Jerusalem and nature's response sets the tone for what is to follow in the proclamations concerning the nations (1:3–2:16).

PROCLAMATIONS CONCERNING THE NATIONS

Amos 1:3–2:16

This first block of material is a collection of proclamations concerning eight centers of Syria Palestine: Damascus (1:3-5), Gaza (1:6-8), Tyre (1:9-10),

Because they threshed Gilead
with sledges of iron,
⁴I will send fire upon the house of
Hazael,
and it will devour the strongholds of Ben-hadad.
⁵I will break the barred gate of
Damascus;

From the Valley of Aven I will cut
off the one enthroned,
And the sceptered ruler from
Beth-eden;
the people of Aram shall be exiled
to Kir, says the LORD.

Edom (1:11-12), Ammon (1:13-15), Moab (2:1-3), Judah (2:4-5), and Israel
(2:6-16). Each proclamation presents heinous examples of violent deeds,
done, in particular, against human beings.

1:3-5 Concerning Aram/Damascus

The first proclamation concerns Aram/Damascus, the capital of Syria.
The passage describes a violent military campaign launched against Gilead,
one of Israel's richest territories, near Damascus. The brutality of the campaign is described with metaphorical language: "they [the people of Da-
mascus] threshed [the people of] Gilead with sledges of iron" (1:3).

Amos makes known that such brutality will not go unchecked; God
promises a fourfold chastisement: (1) to torch the house of Hazael and the
strongholds of Ben-hadad; (2) to break Damascus's gate bars; (3) to cut off
the inhabitants from the Valley of Aven, along with the one who holds the
scepter from Beth-eden; and (4) to exile Aram's people to Kir. Hazael was
the name of an Aramean ruler but here the reference is to the kingdom of
Aram and not to a specific ruler. Ben-hadad is also the name of an Aramean
ruler. Here the reference can be to either a ruler or a dynasty. The exact location of the Valley of Aven is unknown, but Biqaa Valley in present-day
Lebanon is a suggested locale. Beth-eden literally means "house of pleasure" and seems to be Bit-Adini, an Aramean state situated between two
rivers: the upper Euphrates and the Balih. The exact location of Kir is also
unknown, but Mesopotamia is the common consensus among scholars.

The text reveals that Israel's God does not tolerate injustice. The text
portrays an extraordinary power play. Because Damascus oppressed Gilead
violently, Damascus is to reap what it has sown—violence. The poet describes
God as one who will inflict terrible, violent, lethal punishments on Damascus
because of the terrible and violent deed it has done to Gilead. Damascus had
power over Gilead, so God threatens to have *power over* Damascus. God will
win for three reasons: (1) God is the all-powerful, sovereign one who acts on
behalf of those who have been oppressed; (2) the injustice is done to Gilead,
one of Israel's richest territories, and therefore God most certainly will act

Philistia

⁶Thus says the LORD:

For three crimes of Gaza, and now four—
I will not take it back—
Because they exiled an entire population,
handing them over to Edom,
⁷I will send fire upon the wall of Gaza,
and it will devour its strongholds;
⁸From Ashdod I will cut off the one enthroned
and the sceptered ruler from Ashkelon;
I will turn my hand against Ekron,
and the last of the Philistines shall perish,
says the Lord GOD.

---

on behalf of what belongs to God's chosen people, especially since God is Israel's God and this is Israel's story, told from Israel's perspective; and (3) a group of people, expressed collectively through the use of "Damascus," had power over another group of people, so God will indeed have the last word.

In verses 3-5 the poet metaphorically portrays God as "warrior God" who has power over injustice and power over other peoples. As warrior God, God promises to deal with injustice by conquering the enemy, the perpetrator of injustice. In the ancient world, God was imagined as a male deity who was Lord of creation and Lord of history. Furthermore, the historical and cultural times of the prophets were marked by nations in conflict with each other, with Israel being no exception. Consequently, experiences and ideologies of war shaped and informed Israel's self-understanding and poetic expression.

1:6-8 Concerning Philistia

The second proclamation of judgment concerns Gaza, also known as the Philistines. Here the poet uses metonymy: Gaza represents the entire Philistine empire, just as Damascus in verses 3-5 represented all of the Aramean empire. In verse 6, the poet depicts God speaking through the prophet Amos. God accuses Gaza of a crime that it committed against defenseless people: Gaza is guilty of slave trade. Entire communities were carried into exile and handed over to Edom (1:6) so that they could serve the interests of the powerful. Verses 7-8 describe the divine chastisement that will befall Gaza because of its crime. The text depicts the commodification of human beings: people using other people for their own gain, an injustice that existed in the ancient world but also continues today. God is again portrayed as warrior God who will mete out violent punishment to avenge the victims and to strike at the oppressors. As in the oracle against Damascus (1:3-5), the central image of chastisement is fire (1:7). Like verses

Tyre

⁹Thus says the LORD:

For three crimes of Tyre, and
  now four—
I will not take it back—
Because they handed over an
  entire population to
  Edom,
and did not remember their
  covenant of brother-
  hood,
¹⁰I will send fire upon the wall of
  Tyre,
and it will devour its strongholds.

Edom

¹¹Thus says the LORD:

For three crimes of Edom, and
  now four—
I will not take it back—
Because he pursued his brother
  with the sword,
  suppressing all pity,
Persisting in his anger,
  his wrath raging without
  end,
¹²I will send fire upon Teman,
  and it will devour the strongholds of Bozrah.

3-5, the text makes clear that injustice is not divinely sanctioned; the powerful will be brought low; however, the means will be violent just like it will be for Damascus/Aram.

1:9-10 Concerning Tyre

The third proclamation concerns Tyre, the main city of the Phoenicians during the mid-eighth century. This text is similar to the proclamation concerning Gaza insofar as Tyre stands divinely accused for the same crime as Gaza. Added to the issue of human commodification, however, is the fact that Tyre "did not remember their covenant of brotherhood [kinship]" (1:9b). This reference is a poetic way of saying that Tyre disregarded and violated treaties, with the covenant of kinship being the paradigm of all treaties. Such deeds reap divine anger and the promise of divine chastisement. Justice will be done, but how? The motifs, metaphors, and issues of this passage echo those of verses 3-5 and 6-8.

1:11-12 Concerning Edom

In the fourth proclamation Amos declares Edom guilty of piteously pursuing his brother with the sword. Edom is also guilty of harboring anger and wrath relentlessly. Edom has violated the customary ethos of kinship obligations. The divine chastisement is, once again, fire. For the fourth time, the poet emphasizes the fact that injustice will not be tolerated and that God will deal with the issue albeit with violence. Edom included the region beginning in the north at the River Zered and extended southward to the Gulf of Aqabah. Both Bozrah and Teman were important Edomite cities.

Ammon

¹³Thus says the LORD:

> For three crimes of the Am-
>   monites, and now four—
>   I will not take it back—
> Because they ripped open
>   pregnant women in
>   Gilead,
>   in order to extend their
>   territory,
> ¹⁴I will kindle a fire upon the
>   wall of Rabbah,
>   and it will devour its strong-
>   holds
> Amid war cries on the day of
>   battle,
>   amid stormwind on the day
>   of tempest.
> ¹⁵Their king shall go into exile,

> he and his princes with him,
>   says the LORD.

Moab

2 ¹Thus says the LORD:

> For three crimes of Moab, and now
>   four—
>   I will not take it back—
> Because he burned to ashes
>   the bones of Edom's king,
> ²I will send fire upon Moab,
>   and it will devour the strong-
>   holds of Kerioth;
> Moab shall meet death amid
>   uproar,
>   battle cries and blasts of the
>   ram's horn.
> ³I will cut off the ruler from its
>   midst,

1:13-15 Concerning Ammon

Perhaps one of the most gruesome and violent images in the collection of proclamations concerning the nations is directed against the Ammonites. These people are descendants of Ben-Ammi, Lot's son. Their land was located in the area north and east of Moab. The Ammonites are guilty of ripping open pregnant women in Gilead for selfish reasons: to enlarge their own territory. This atrocity represents the abuse of power and war at its worst. Additionally, women, children, and the poor were considered to be among the most vulnerable members of the society of their day. Amos makes clear to the Ammonites that the punishment threatened will be as violent as the crime itself. Unbridled, selfish human power is checked by divine power but, according to the text, the power exercised is violent and destructive. Lastly, in verses 13-15 power is portrayed as a violent and oppressive force, whether it is exercised unjustly or justly.

2:1-3 Concerning Moab

The repetitious recital of the nations' injustices continues in Amos 2:1-3, the sixth proclamation that is addressed to Moab. The region itself is primarily a high plateau with mountainous areas and deep gorges. Once controlled by Israel before the Moabites gained their independence, the land and its people were later conquered by the Assyrians in 735 B.C. and by invading Arabs in 650 B.C. Moab is guilty of burning to lime the royal

and all the princes I will slay
   with him, says the LORD.

Judah

⁴Thus says the LORD:

   For three crimes of Judah, and
      now four—
   I will not take it back—

Because they spurned the
      instruction of the LORD,
   and did not keep his statutes;
Because the lies which their
      ancestors followed
   have led them astray,
⁵I will send fire upon Judah,
   and it will devour the strong-
      holds of Jerusalem.

---

bones of the king of Edom. Burning the bones of a human being was considered a severe desecration, especially since within the culture at this time
such an act was reserved for the most despicable of criminals (see, e.g., Gen
38:24; Lev 20:14; 21:9). As in the other proclamations, Amos makes clear
that such a deed is unacceptable, especially to God, who promises to send
fire upon Moab, to cut off the ruler from its midst, and to kill all its officials
with him.

Amos's proclamation presents a devastating picture indeed. First, it
shows the lack of reverence on the part of some people for the remains of
another. Second, the punishment that God promises is similar to that of the
other texts—fire—and yet, the chastisement is even more lethal. God promises to cut off Moab's ruler from its midst and to kill all Moab's officials
with him. Again, God's promised response to violence is violence, and,
once more, we see how the prophet's message reflects the violent culture
of the day, whereby God has to be depicted as one stronger than all the
enemy nations and their gods if Israel's God is to be understood as "sovereign" and reigning over all gods, all leaders, and all forces.

2:4-5 Concerning Judah

This proclamation concerning Judah is different from the other proclamations concerning the nations. Judah's crime involves no explicit use of power
or use of any violence. Rather, Judah has rejected God's law and has gone
astray, which is a most egregious offense because torah is connected to the
nation's ethical conduct. Forgetfulness of God leads to forgetfulness of God's
ways, which, in turn, leads to political, social, economic, and religious dis-
order and dysfunction. Judah is in complete disarray prior to the nation's
complete collapse in 587 B.C. when it was invaded by the Babylonians.

The imagery of fire used in verse 5 reflects the violence of warfare common to Judah, particularly during the eighth to sixth centuries B.C. When
used in association with God, fire contributes to the image of a God of wrath
who desires to use power to demolish a nation even when that nation has

Israel

⁶Thus says the LORD:
For three crimes of Israel, and
now four—
I will not take it back—
Because they hand over the just
for silver,
and the poor for a pair of
sandals;
⁷They trample the heads of the
destitute
into the dust of the earth,
and force the lowly out of the
way.
Son and father sleep with the same
girl,
profaning my holy name.
⁸Upon garments taken in pledge
they recline beside any altar.
Wine at treasury expense
they drink in their temples.
⁹Yet it was I who destroyed the
Amorites before them,
who were as tall as cedars,
and as strong as oak trees.
I destroyed their fruit above
and their roots beneath.
¹⁰It was I who brought you up from
the land of Egypt,
and who led you through the
desert for forty years,
to occupy the land of the
Amorites;
¹¹I who raised up prophets among
your children,
and nazirites among your
young men.
Is this not so, Israelites?—
oracle of the LORD.
¹²But you made the nazirites drink
wine,
and commanded the prophets,
"Do not prophesy!"
¹³Look, I am groaning beneath you,
as a wagon groans when laden
with sheaves.
¹⁴Flight shall elude the swift,
and the strong shall not retain
strength;
The warrior shall not save his life,
¹⁵nor shall the archer stand his
ground;
The swift of foot shall not escape,
nor shall the horseman save his
life.
¹⁶And the most stouthearted of
warriors
shall flee naked on that day—
oracle of the LORD.

not been indicted for any explicit violent crime. Amos's depiction of God makes clear that God makes no distinctions between the expressions of indictment and their respective punishments. All receive the same threat—fire (1:4, 7, 10, 12, 14; 2:2, 5).

2:6-16 Concerning Israel

In the proclamation concerning Israel, one sees God, through Amos, enumerating the many transgressions of the nation. Each transgression, in some way, is a violation against other people. First, some Israelites are guilty of the economic exploitation of the righteous and needy (2:6). Second, the poor suffer abuse (2:7). Third, the lowly are pushed "out of the way"; in other words, they are denied access to and deprived of fair treatment by the court systems (2:7; see also Isa 3:15 and Prov 22:22 for the abuse of the poor and deprivation of their rights). Fourth, two men—a son and a father—

III. Threefold Summons to Hear the Word of the Lord

First Summons

3 ¹Hear this word, Israelites, that the LORD speaks concerning you,

concerning the whole family I brought up from the land of Egypt:
²You alone I have known, among all the families of the earth;

---

sexually exploited a maiden (2:7). Fifth, debtors are exploited, perhaps poor men and widows specifically (2:8). Law codes restricted the taking of certain items for collateral and also set limits on how long something could be kept. For example, a widow's garment could not be taken from her (Deut 24:17) nor could a poor person's cloak be kept overnight (Exod 22:25-27; Deut 24:12-13). Sixth, others are drinking in holy places the wine that was obtained from fines they imposed, perhaps on the poor (2:8b). Some Israelites are also guilty of making the Nazirites drink wine, thus forcing them to break one of their vows of consecration (see Judg 13:14-15; Num 6:3-4); others silence the prophets (2:12).

Amos exposes an abuse of power on the part of some of the Israelite people. The victims of such abuse, for the most part, are the righteous, the poor, women, and people following a holy way of life. Within Israelite society, these people would be the most vulnerable in terms of political, social, economic, and religious status, and therefore the people most easily abused. The idea of making the Nazirites drink wine and commanding the prophets not to prophesy admits of a certain overt disregard for the explicit honoring of God. Through this proclamation Amos makes clear that the threads of power, domination, and control were part of the fabric of Israelite society.

In verses 13-16 the poet describes God's response. God will come as a foe among those who stepped all over the vulnerable, and God will push them down.

THREE WORDS TO ISRAEL

Amos 3:1–5:6, 8-9

This second block of material consists of "three words" to Israel. Each one of the three units begins with "Hear this word" (3:1; 4:1; 5:1), followed by a series of proclamations that reveal Israel's waywardness, how God plans on chastising Israel for its transgressions, and how God has already chastised Israel to no avail since Israel has not returned to God. The passages also shed light on Creator God's power (5:8-9). This God remains faithfully committed to Israel despite Israel's shortcomings (5:5, 14).

Therefore I will punish you
for all your iniquities.

³Do two journey together
unless they have agreed?
⁴Does a lion roar in the forest
when it has no prey?
Does a young lion cry out from its
den
unless it has seized something?
⁵Does a bird swoop down on a trap
on the ground
when there is no lure for it?
Does a snare spring up from the
ground
without catching anything?
⁶Does the ram's horn sound in a city
without the people becoming
frightened?

Does disaster befall a city
unless the Lord has caused it?

⁷(Indeed, the Lord God does nothing
without revealing his plan to his servants the prophets.)

⁸The lion has roared,
who would not fear?
The Lord God has spoken,
who would not prophesy?

⁹Proclaim this in the strongholds of
Assyria,
in the strongholds of the land of
Egypt:
"Gather on the mount of Samaria,
and see the great disorders
within it,

3:1-15 First word

God's first word to Israel begins on a poignant yet stern note. In verses 1-2 the poet depicts God as being completely frustrated with Israel. Israel shares a special relationship with God, having been rescued from Egyptian slavery by God and having been "known" intimately by God better than all the other families of the earth, and yet, Israel does not turn back to God and does not turn from iniquity.

Verses 3-6 feature a series of rhetorical questions to support the point being made by God in verse 7, namely, that God does, in fact, make known divine plans and intentions before events happen. Through the prophet Amos, and other prophets as well, Israel has been informed of its wrong-doings and has been forewarned about the consequences that will follow. Verses 8-10 bear these points out. Verse 8 features two more rhetorical questions with an implied metaphor that compares God to a lion who has indeed roared/spoken. The word to be proclaimed is revealed in verses 9-10. The prophet is to make known to Assyria and Egypt—Israel's ene-mies—Israel's wickedness and oppression. Thus, both Assyria and Egypt will be made aware of Israel's discord and lack of unity, which leaves the kingdom ripe for invasion. Following the detailing of transgression is an announcement of judgment in verse 11. The foreshadowed destructive enemy will be Assyria, though Amos never mentions Assyria in his speeches. Isaiah, Amos's contemporary, does mention Assyria as the rod of God's anger that God sends forth (see Isa 10:5). Israel has now been

the oppressions within its
midst."
[10]They do not know how to do
what is right—
oracle of the LORD—
Storing up in their strongholds
violence and destruction.
[11]Therefore thus says the Lord GOD:
An enemy shall surround the land,
tear down your fortresses,
and pillage your strongholds.
[12]Thus says the LORD:
As the shepherd rescues from the
mouth of the lion
a pair of sheep's legs or the tip
of an ear,
So shall the Israelites escape,
those who dwell in Samaria,
With the corner of a couch
or a piece of a cot.

[13]Hear and bear witness against the
house of Jacob—

an oracle of the Lord GOD, the
God of hosts:
[14]On the day when I punish Israel
for its crimes,
I will also punish the altars of
Bethel;
The horns of the altar shall be broken off
and fall to the ground.
[15]I will strike the winter house
and the summer house;
The houses of ivory shall lie in ruin,
and their many rooms shall be
no more—
oracle of the LORD.

Second Summons

4 [1]Hear this word, you cows of Bashan,
who live on the mount of
Samaria:
Who oppress the destitute
and abuse the needy;

---

forewarned (cf. 3:7). Israel, and specifically those who dwell in the capital city of Samaria, will not be completely destroyed. A small group—a remnant—will survive the invasion. Here the poet uses a shepherd-lion metaphor. God, as shepherd, will rescue some of the Israelite people from the clutches of the Assyrians, the lion. Lion God in verse 8 will now act as a shepherd, but lion God will also act as a lion in the guise of the Assyrians. Thus, the imagery and metaphorical language in verses 8-12 are rich and multilayered.

Verses 13-15 begin a new proclamation of judgment. To whom the proclamation is addressed is unknown. The anonymous addressee is given a double imperative: to hear (cf. 3:1, 9; 4:1; 5:1) and to witness. The one speaking is the Lord God, the God of hosts, hence, the commander-in-chief of all earthly and heavenly forces. The Israelites are now forewarned again about the divine consequences that they will have to endure because of their transgressions. Their sacred precincts will be destroyed, symbolized by the reference to the altars of Bethel (3:14), and the magnificent residences of the upper wealthy class living in Samaria (cf. 3:9, 12) will be destroyed. Thus, the people will no longer enjoy a life of feasting and prosperity. Israel no longer lives under promise; Israel lives under threat.

Who say to your husbands,
  "Bring us a drink!"
²The Lord GOD has sworn by his
    holiness:
Truly days are coming upon you
    when they shall drag you away
      with ropes,
    your children with fishhooks;
³You shall go out through the
      breached walls
    one in front of the other,
And you shall be exiled to
      Harmon—
    oracle of the LORD.

⁴Come to Bethel and sin,
    to Gilgal and sin all the more!
Each morning bring your sacrifices,
    every third day your tithes;
⁵Burn leavened bread as a thanks-
      giving sacrifice,
    proclaim publicly your volun-
      tary offerings,

For so you love to do, Israelites—
    oracle of the Lord GOD.

⁶Though I made your teeth
    clean of food in all your cities,
    and made bread scarce in all
      your dwellings,
Yet you did not return to me—
    oracle of the LORD.
⁷And I withheld the rain from you
    when the harvest was still three
      months away;
I sent rain upon one city
    but not upon another;
One field was watered by rain,
    but the one I did not water dried
      up;
⁸Two or three cities staggered to
      another to drink water
    but were not satisfied;
Yet you did not return to me—
    oracle of the LORD.

4:1-13 Second word

In Amos 4:1-5 the prophet addresses a group of women of Samaria, the pampered darlings of society in Israel's royalist culture. Amos scorns these women because they appear to be guilty of ruthless exploitation of the poor. Perhaps they were not the direct perpetrators of oppression, but as Amos's proclamation shows, they enjoyed a certain type of lifestyle that was due to economic gain received through their husbands (4:1).

As a response to such a situation, Amos announces that God will deal with the situation. These cows of Bashan will be lifted up with hooks and then roasted! Then they will be carried off without any difficulty to Harmon; they will be deported (4:2-3). Amos continues his biting invective in verses 4-5, one of the strongest condemnations of the official cult as sinful, but this time the address is to all the Israelites who practice rites at Bethal and Gilgal, the two major cult sights in Northern Israel. Amos encourages them to sin there so as to exaggerate their corruption. With tongue in cheek, God, speaking through Amos, challenges the Israelites to transgress and even to multiply transgressions while they simultaneously engage in ritual activities (4:4-5a). Verse 5b closes the unit and captures the entire sentiment of divine condemnation. Thus, Amos exposes the disparity between the people's worship and their way of living.

⁹I struck you with blight and
mildew;
locusts devoured your gardens
and vineyards,
the caterpillar consumed your
fig trees and olive trees;
Yet you did not return to me—
oracle of the LORD.

¹⁰I sent upon you pestilence like
that of Egypt;
with the sword I killed your
young men and your
captured horses,
and to your nostrils I brought
the stench of your camps;
Yet you did not return to me—
oracle of the LORD.

In ancient Israel metaphors provided a foundation for thought and practice in its daily experience and in its religion. The use of metaphors that came from the agricultural world was not uncommon. The Israelites were a people of the land, and many were engaged in animal husbandry. Herds and flocks became the dominant source of metaphors and, thus, their metaphors came from and are reflective of their lived experience. Bovine metaphors were used to express Israel's relationship with God: Israel as a faithful servant is a heifer (Hos 10:11), and a stubborn one at that sometimes (Hos 4:16).

Bashan in Amos 4:1 refers to that plain in Transjordan. It was a famous, lush pasture country (Mic 7:14; Jer 50:19; and Deut 32:14), and its cattle were called "fatlings" (Ezek 39:18). Bashan connoted quality of lifestyle and quality of life. When Amos compares the pampered women of Samaria to the well-fed and pleasantly plump bovines, he introduces the element of imagination and surprise into his oracle. With this metaphor, he makes the point that these women tend to their own self-indulgence, irrespective of the cost to others. Thus, Amos uncovers the role of Samaria's women in the social dynamics of the state's economic aristocracy. They had grown fat on the plunder of the poor and, always wanting more, they hassle their husbands, whom Amos ironically calls "lords," for fresh "drinks"—new acts of injustice. Here, the men appear to be as servants of the women. Thus, with metaphorical language drawn from the culture of his day that appeals to the readers of his day, Amos launches his attack. For his listeners and readers then and now, his point is clear.

The poetic story told in verses 6-13 presents a startling picture. God reiterates all the divinely initiated negative actions that were done against Israel in the hope that Israel would return to God (4:6-13). God withheld rain, struck the people with blight and mildew, laid waste their gardens, had the caterpillar devour fig and olive trees, sent out pestilence, killed the young men with the sword, carried away the people's horses, made a stench go up the people's noses, and overthrew some of them.

¹¹I overthrew you
>as when God overthrew Sodom
>>and Gomorrah;
>you were like a brand plucked
>>from the fire,
>Yet you did not return to me—
>>oracle of the LORD.
¹²Therefore thus I will do to you,
>Israel:
>and since I will deal thus with
>>you,
>prepare to meet your God,
>>O Israel!

¹³The one who forms mountains
>and creates winds,
>and declares to mortals their
>>thoughts;
Who makes dawn into darkness
>and strides upon the heights of
>>the earth,
>the LORD, the God of hosts, is
>>his name!

Third Summons

5 ¹Hear this word which I utter concerning you,
>this dirge, house of Israel:

In the ancient Israelite world, God's blessing meant fertility, longevity, and prosperity, and God's curse meant famines, plagues, and pestilences. If the people had a lush harvest and plenty of good rain, then they had done something right. If they experienced famine and drought, then they had done something wrong. It was also thought that God would strike the land and other elements in the natural world in order to punish the people for their transgressions. If the grapevines withered by the power of God, then the people had no wine. If pestilence struck a crop of corn, then people had no food. Supposedly, then, they would, in their need, return to God and reform their ways. The text of Amos 4:6-13 reflects these attitudes and beliefs.

In verses 6-10 the poet portrays God as intentionally manipulating various elements in the natural world in a destructive way so as to coax the Israelite people to return to God. The God who once saw the natural world as "good" now turns it into a pawn in an effort to turn human beings from their wretched ways. Of importance here is the fact that nature is affected by Yahweh's punitive deeds because Israel is stubborn. And the question arises, should the land and the gifts of nature be used to incur chastisement?

Even human beings are sacrificed in the course of God's action (4:10-11). Such punitive actions, however, do not succeed in having the people turn back to God. In this regard, the text becomes prophetic on another level: neither punitive measures nor violence succeeds in changing hearts needed for the reform and transformation of attitudes and life.

5:1-6, 8-9 Third word

This third word concerning Israel is as ominous as the other two words. The first unit (5:1-2) takes the form of a dirge that describes the house of

²She is fallen, to rise no more,
  virgin Israel;
She lies abandoned on her land,
  with no one to raise her up.
³For thus says the Lord GOD
  to the house of Israel:
The city that marched out with a
    thousand
  shall be left with a hundred,
Another that marched out with a
    hundred
  shall be left with ten.
⁴For thus says the LORD
  to the house of Israel:
Seek me, that you may live,
⁵but do not seek Bethel;
Do not come to Gilgal,
  and do not cross over to
    Beer-sheba;
For Gilgal shall be led into exile
  and Bethel shall be no more.

⁶Seek the LORD, that you may live,
  lest he flare up against the house
    of Joseph like a fire
  that shall consume the house of
    Israel, with no one to
    quench it.

⁸The one who made the Pleiades
    and Orion,
  who turns darkness into dawn,
  and darkens day into night;
Who summons the waters of the
    sea,
  and pours them out on the sur-
    face of the earth;
⁹Who makes destruction fall
    suddenly upon the strong-
    hold
  and brings ruin upon the
    fortress,
  the LORD is his name.

Israel as if it had already fallen with no hope of being restored. What follows are two more proclamations, verse 3 and verses 4-9, both of which begin with the traditional prophetic messenger formula "thus says the LORD" (5:3, 4) that lends credence and authority to what the prophet is about to proclaim. In verse 3 the prophet foreshadows the losses that Israel is about to experience during the Assyrian invasion. In the midst of such impending devastation, hope abounds: not all of the people will perish (cf. 3:12).

In verses 4-6 the poet features God speaking through the prophet. The Israelite people are being exhorted to seek God so that they may live (5:4; cf. 5:6). They are encouraged not to seek Bethel, not to come to Gilgal, and not to cross over to Beer-sheba. Bethel is about nineteen kilometers (twelve miles) north of Jerusalem. After the death of Solomon and during the time of Jeroboam, Bethel became a leading center of idolatry (1 Kgs 13:1-32; 2 Kgs 10:29) and the main sanctuary of Israel (see Amos 7:13). As a religious center, Bethel rivaled the temple in Jerusalem. Like Bethel, Gilgal became a center of idolatry and was condemned not only by Amos but also by his contemporary, Hosea (see Hos 4:15). Gilgal is about one mile northeast of Jericho. The reference to "house of Joseph" is synonymous with "house of Israel" (5:6).

IV. Three Woes

First Woe

⁷Woe to those who turn justice into wormwood
and cast righteousness to the ground,
¹⁰They hate those who reprove at the gate
and abhor those who speak with integrity;
¹¹Therefore, because you tax the destitute
and exact from them levies of grain,
Though you have built houses of hewn stone,
you shall not live in them;
Though you have planted choice vineyards,
you shall not drink their wine.
¹²Yes, I know how many are your crimes,

how grievous your sins:
Oppressing the just, accepting bribes,
turning away the needy at the gate.
¹³(Therefore at this time the wise are struck dumb
for it is an evil time.)

¹⁴Seek good and not evil,
that you may live;
Then truly the LORD, the God of hosts,
will be with you as you claim.
¹⁵Hate evil and love good,
and let justice prevail at the gate;
Then it may be that the LORD, the God of hosts,
will have pity on the remnant of Joseph.

¹⁶Therefore, thus says the LORD,
the God of hosts, the Lord:

Verses 8-9 establish the credibility and power of Israel's God, who is not only Lord of creation but also Lord of history. This God, who made the stars and galaxies, who summoned sea waters and poured them out over the earth, who brought destruction and ruin, is named LORD.

THREE WOES

Amos 5:7, 10-17; 5:18-27; 6:1-14

Three woe proclamations comprised the third block of material in this next section of the book of Amos. Israel stands condemned for its duplicitous religious rituals. The people worship God in solemn assemblies, offer choice offerings, and yet they neglect the weightier matters of the law, namely, justice and righteousness. Israel's elite also stand condemned for their self-centered, self-indulgent luxurious lifestyle.

5:7, 10-17 First woe

In Amos 5:7, 10-17 the poet casts the first woe proclamation. The central issue is Israel's neglect of justice, righteousness, and truth. In verses 10-13 the prophet condemns the Israelites for those practices that break covenant

In every square there shall be
lamentation,
and in every street they shall
cry, "Oh, no!"
They shall summon the farmers to
wail
and the professional mourners
to lament.
¹⁷And in every vineyard there shall
be lamentation
when I pass through your midst,
says the LORD.

Second Woe

¹⁸Woe to those who yearn
for the day of the LORD!
What will the day of the LORD
mean for you?
It will be darkness, not light!
¹⁹As if someone fled from a lion
and a bear met him;
Or as if on entering the house
he rested his hand against the
wall,
and a snake bit it.

²⁰Truly, the day of the LORD will be
darkness, not light,
gloom without any brightness!

²¹I hate, I despise your feasts,
I take no pleasure in your
solemnities.
²²Even though you bring me your
burnt offerings and grain
offerings
I will not accept them;
Your stall-fed communion
offerings,
I will not look upon them.
²³Take away from me
your noisy songs;
The melodies of your harps,
I will not listen to them.
²⁴Rather let justice surge like
waters,
and righteousness like an unfailing stream.
²⁵Did you bring me sacrifices and
grain offerings
for forty years in the desert, O
house of Israel?

and exploit neighbors. Earlier, the people were called to seek God; now, they are being called to "[s]eek good and not evil" (5:14). Some among the Israelites are guilty of the inordinate assertion of power. Once again, the poor (5:11), the righteous (5:12), and the needy (5:12) are overpowered and become victims of a whole array of injustices. Yet, God will deliver justice.

5:18-27 Second woe

One of the most gut-wrenching proclamations in the book of Amos is, perhaps, 5:18-27. In verses 18-20, the poet depicts God questioning the Israelites about why they are anticipating the Day of the Lord. This day was, at one point, a positive and liberating time as in the day when Israel was freed from Egyptian bondage. Now, however, the Day of the Lord will be the complete opposite of what the Israelites expect.

In Amos 5:21-24 divine dissatisfaction with the Israelites' rituals is expressed again. Here, God states boldly, "I hate, I despise your feasts, / I

▶ This symbol indicates a cross-reference number in the *Catechism of the Catholic Church*. See page 145 for number citations.

²⁶Yet you will carry away Sukuth,
    your king,
and Kaiwan, your star-image,
    your gods that you have made
        for yourselves,
²⁷As I exile you beyond Damascus,
    says the LORD,
    whose name is the God of hosts.

Third Woe

6 ¹Woe to those who are complacent
    in Zion,
    secure on the mount of Samaria,
Leaders of the first among nations,
    to whom the people of Israel turn.
²Pass over to Calneh and see,
    go from there to Hamath the
        great,
    and down to Gath of the
        Philistines.

Are you better than these
    kingdoms,
    or is your territory greater than
        theirs?
³You who would put off the day of
    disaster,
    yet hasten the time of violence!
⁴Those who lie on beds of ivory,
    and lounge upon their couches;
Eating lambs taken from the flock,
    and calves from the stall;
⁵Who improvise to the music of the
    harp,
    composing on musical
        instruments like David,
⁶Who drink wine from bowls,
    and anoint themselves with the
        best oils,
    but are not made ill by the
        collapse of Joseph;

---

take no pleasure in your solemnities" (5:21). Moreover, God rejects the people's burnt offerings, grain offerings, and well-being offerings (5:22). After requesting that all song and music be silenced (5:23), God then calls for justice to "surge like waters, / and righteousness like an unfailing stream" (5:24). Without a doubt, Amos makes the point that God could not care less about the people's offerings and sacrifices, especially when they are being made by a people sunk in the mire of transgression. What God desires is justice and righteousness, hence, right relationships that embrace the spirit of torah with its vision for love and its call to an ethical way of life.

6:1-14 Third woe

In Amos 6:1-14 the prophet rails against those who are complacent in Zion and secure in Samaria (6:1-7). Although the text gives no mention of the economic status of these people, one can presume that the prophet is delivering a woe proclamation to the wealthy upper class of Israelite society (cf. 4:1, 4-7) that, by its complacent and self-indulgent attitude, allows violence to go unchecked (6:3). Would that they had used their power on behalf of justice, but this seems not to have been their choice (6:4-7).

In verses 8-10, the prophet upbraids the Israelites for their pride, a theme that continues in verses 11-14, where they stand condemned for turning justice into poison and righteousness into wormwood, and for taking pride in their own strength without due recognition of God's role in their recent

⁷Therefore, now they shall be the
first to go into exile,
and the carousing of those who
lounged shall cease.

⁸The Lord GOD has sworn by his
very self—
an oracle of the LORD, the God
of hosts:
I abhor the pride of Jacob,
I hate his strongholds,
and I will hand over the city
with everything in it;
⁹Should there remain ten people
in a single house, these shall die.
¹⁰When a relative or one who
prepares the body picks up
the remains
to carry them out of the house,
If he says to someone in the
recesses of the house,
"Is anyone with you?" and the
answer is, "No one,"
Then he shall say, "Silence!"

for no one must mention the
name of the LORD.
¹¹Indeed, the LORD has given the
command
to shatter the great house to bits,
and reduce the small house to
rubble.
¹²Can horses run over rock,
or can one plow the sea with
oxen?
Yet you have turned justice into gall,
and the fruit of righteousness
into wormwood,
¹³You who rejoice in Lodebar,
and say, "Have we not, by our
own strength,
seized Karnaim for ourselves?"
¹⁴Look, I am raising up against you,
house of Israel—
oracle of the LORD, the God of
hosts—
A nation that shall oppress you
from Lebo-hamath even to the
Wadi Arabah.

---

successful military campaign (6:12b-13). The Israelite people are, therefore, guilty of proud self-assertion and a perversion of justice. However, are all of them guilty, as the text would have the reader believe? Underlying their pride and perversion is the use of power to obstruct and to oppress. To suppress such attitudes, God promises to raise up a nation that will oppress the house of Israel itself. Similar to other texts from Amos, this passage portrays a hierarchical power play that begins and ends with oppression. Additionally, God's power and control comes to the fore: God will use one nation to oppress another. This text reflects attitudes endemic to both patriarchy and hierarchy, characteristic of the culture of the day and attitudes that were likely shared by both the prophet's own theological consciousness and message as well as those of the texts' later editors.

FIVE VISIONS; TWO JUDGMENT SPEECHES

Amos 7:1–9:10

In addition to a series of "three words" and "three woes," the book of Amos also contains five visions (7:1-3, 4-6, 7-9; 8:1-3; 9:1-10), whereby the

V. Symbolic Visions

First Vision: The Locust Swarm

7 ¹This is what the Lord GOD showed me: He was forming a locust swarm when the late growth began to come up (the late growth after the king's mowing). ²When they had finished eating the grass in the land, I said:

Forgive, O Lord GOD!
Who will raise up Jacob?
He is so small!

³The LORD relented concerning this. "This shall not be," said the Lord GOD.

Second Vision: The Rain of Fire

⁴This is what the Lord GOD showed me: He was summoning a rain of fire. It had devoured the great abyss and was consuming the fields. ⁵Then I said:

Cease, O Lord GOD!
Who will raise up Jacob?
He is so small!

⁶The LORD relented concerning this. "This also shall not be," said the Lord GOD.

Third Vision: The Plummet

⁷This is what the Lord GOD showed me: He was standing, plummet in hand, by a wall built with a plummet. ⁸The Lord GOD asked me, "What do you see, Amos?" And I answered, "A plummet." Then the LORD said:

---

prophet warns the Israelites of what is about to befall them. Each vision opens with the words "This is what the Lord GOD showed me" (7:1, 4, 7; 8:1), with the exception of the fifth one, which is a vision of God and the destruction of the sanctuary.

7:1-3 First vision: locust

The first vision announces the coming of a swarm of locusts. Locusts are grasshoppers. Their eggs hatch in the springtime, and their shells turn brown from larval friction when they swarm together. In this passage, they represent an uncontrollable agricultural disaster that was due to occur at the second grain and hay growth in the month of April after the times of the "latter rains." The fruit of this second planting was reserved for the farmers themselves who depended on it for themselves, their families, and their livestock. Amos foresees a land soon to be devoid of vegetation (cf. Deut 28:42). Such a vision causes the prophet to make intercession to God on behalf of the sinful people, and God responds favorably.

7:4-6 Second vision: fire

The description of the second vision is similar in pattern to the first vision. This vision of fire recalls Deuteronomy 32:22. The people and their livestock will be left starving. Again Amos makes intercession and God relents.

See, I am laying the plummet
    in the midst of my people Israel;
    I will forgive them no longer.
⁹The high places of Isaac shall be
        laid waste,
    and the sanctuaries of Israel
        made desolate;
    and I will attack the house of
        Jeroboam with the sword.

Biographical Interlude: Amos and Amaziah

¹⁰Amaziah, the priest of Bethel, sent word to Jeroboam, king of Israel: "Amos has conspired against you within the house of Israel; the country cannot endure all his words. ¹¹For this is what Amos says:

'Jeroboam shall die by the sword,
    and Israel shall surely be exiled
        from its land.'"

¹²To Amos, Amaziah said: "Off with you, seer, flee to the land of Judah and there earn your bread by prophesying!

¹³But never again prophesy in Bethel; for it is the king's sanctuary and a royal temple." ¹⁴Amos answered Amaziah, "I am not a prophet, nor do I belong to a company of prophets. I am a herdsman and a dresser of sycamores, ¹⁵but the Lord took me from following the flock, and the Lord said to me, 'Go, prophesy to my people Israel.' ¹⁶Now hear the word of the Lord:

You say: 'Do not prophesy against
        Israel,
    do not preach against the house
        of Isaac.'
¹⁷Therefore thus says the Lord:
Your wife shall become a prostitute
        in the city,
    and your sons and daughters
        shall fall by the sword.
Your land shall be parcelled out by
        measuring line,
    and you yourself shall die in an
        unclean land;
    and Israel shall be exiled from
        its land."

7:7-9 Third vision: the plummet

In this vision the prophet sees a plummet that God will lay in the midst of the people. A plummet is a small heavy weight at the end of a long cord. Israel's destruction is imminent, particularly for the sanctuaries.

7:10-17 First judgment speech concerning Amaziah, his family, and Israel

Nestled in between the vision reports is a biographical interlude that outlines a dispute between Amos and Amaziah, the priest of Bethel. Amaziah sets up Amos in an attempt to silence him because Amos's word is challenging and uncomfortable. Amaziah, however, is unsuccessful, and Amos's prophecy is later directed against the priest!

8:1-3 Fourth vision: summer fruit

This fourth vision of end-of-the-summer fruit symbolizes that Israel's end is near, and this time God will no longer forgive the people.

Fourth Vision: The Summer Fruit

8 ¹This is what the Lord God showed me: a basket of end-of-summer fruit. ²He asked, "What do you see, Amos?" And I answered, "A basket of end-of-summer fruit." And the Lord said to me:

> The end has come for my people
>   Israel;
>   I will forgive them no longer.
> ³The temple singers will wail on
>   that day—
>   oracle of the Lord God.
> Many shall be the corpses,
>   strewn everywhere—Silence!

> ⁴Hear this, you who trample upon
>   the needy
>   and destroy the poor of the land:
> ⁵"When will the new moon be
>   over," you ask,
>   "that we may sell our grain,
> And the sabbath,
>   that we may open the grain-bins?
> We will diminish the ephah,
>   add to the shekel,
>   and fix our scales for cheating!

> ⁶We will buy the destitute for silver,
>   and the poor for a pair of sandals;
>   even the worthless grain we will
>   sell!"
> ⁷The Lord has sworn by the pride
>   of Jacob:
>   Never will I forget a thing they
>   have done!
> ⁸Shall not the land tremble because
>   of this,
>   and all who dwell in it mourn?
> It will all rise up and toss like the
>   Nile,
>   and subside like the river of
>   Egypt.
> ⁹On that day—oracle of the Lord
>   God—
>   I will make the sun set at
>   midday
>   and in broad daylight cover the
>   land with darkness.
> ¹⁰I will turn your feasts into
>   mourning
>   and all your songs into dirges.
> I will cover the loins of all with
>   sackcloth
>   and make every head bald.

8:4-14 Second judgment speech concerning Israel's unjust inhabitants

One of the more vivid passages that describe social injustice within the Israelite community is Amos 8:4-8. In this passage, Amos—direct and unrestrained—addresses a group of Israelites who have acted unethically on several counts. First, they have exploited the poor economically (8:5; cf. 2:6ff.; 4:1; 5:10-13). Torah insists that the Israelites care for the poor and the most vulnerable ones in the society. Second, those doing the exploiting also are selling the sweepings of wheat from their harvests (8:5). This injustice done to the poor is a violation of torah, which insists that the gleanings of the harvest were to be left for the poor (Lev 19:9-10; 23:22). Third, the poor are made into bartered goods in human trade traffic (8:6). Such reprehensible behavior on the part of those possessing greater economic and social advantage and know-how does not go unnoticed. In verses 7-14, God plans to take action against the culprits of injustice whose ruthlessness stems from apostasy and greed (8:5, 13-14).

I will make it like the time of
    mourning for an only child,
and its outcome like a day of
    bitter weeping.
    ¹¹See, days are coming—oracle of
    the Lord GOD—
    when I will send a famine upon
    the land:
Not a hunger for bread, or a thirst
    for water,
but for hearing the word of the
    LORD.
¹²They shall stagger from sea to sea
and wander from north to east

In search of the word of the LORD,
    but they shall not find it.
¹³On that day, beautiful young
    women and young men
    shall faint from thirst,
¹⁴Those who swear by Ashima of
    Samaria,
and who say, "By the life of your
    god, O Dan,"
"By the life of the Power of
    Beer-sheba!"
They shall fall, never to rise
    again.

In verses 7-14, and specifically in verses 9-14, the poet next depicts God's wrath as an earthquake. Retributive measures include the sun going down, feasts turning into mourning and songs into lamentations (8:9-10), sackcloth covering the loins and shaved heads (8:10bc), people deprived of hearing God's words with a resultant aimlessness in their lives (8:11-12), and famine adversely affecting the people (8:13). Injustice will not go without reprimand; unethical behavior is unacceptable.

Similar to Amos 4:6-13, social injustice affected not only human life but also nonhuman life, and, by extension, all creation. For Israel, sin and suffering were linked. According to their worldview, understood and interpreted by their religious imagination that interacted with their life experience, infidelity to God, the breaking of the covenant, and the forgetfulness and transgression of torah led to punitive divine chastisement in the name of justice. Thus, in various prophetic texts, readers hear and see references to the suffering of the natural world, and, specifically, the suffering of the land, as a direct result of God's action. In essence, it was thought that God would or did strike the land in order to punish the people, in an effort to reestablish justice and to woo them back to God through their repentance. Hence, if the land experienced a drought or flood, crops would be destroyed and the people would suffer. Furthermore, when Israel did lose its land to foreign countries, this was also understood as either sanctioned or ordained by God because of the people's transgressions.

In Amos 8:4-14 the poet reveals to people then and now that in a hierarchical society, power is, in fact, connected to one's social and economic status. This power can be used—and many times is—abusively for self-serving purposes that deny others their legal rights and/or human dignity.

Fifth Vision: The Destruction of the Sanctuary

9 ¹I saw the Lord standing beside the altar. And he said:

Strike the capitals
  so that the threshold shakes!
  Break them off on the heads of
    them all!
Those who are left I will slay with
  the sword.
Not one shall get away,
  no survivor shall escape.
²Though they dig down to Sheol,
  even from there my hand shall
    take them;
Though they climb to the heavens,
  even from there I shall bring
    them down.
³Though they hide on the summit
  of Carmel,
  there too I will hunt them down
    and take them;
Though they hide from my gaze at
  the bottom of the sea,
  there I will command the
    serpent to bite them.

⁴Though they go into captivity
  before their enemies,
  there I will command the sword
    to slay them.
I will fix my gaze upon them
  for evil and not for good.

⁵The Lord GOD of hosts,
Who melts the earth with his touch,
  so that all who dwell on it
    mourn,
So that it will all rise up like the
  Nile,
  and subside like the river of
    Egypt;
⁶Who has built his upper chamber
  in heaven,
  and established his vault over
    the earth;
Who summons the waters of the sea
  and pours them upon the
    surface of the earth—
  the LORD is his name.

⁷Are you not like the Ethiopians to
  me,
  O Israelites?—oracle of the
    LORD—

Yet, this sort of domination will not have the last word; justice will be done. God's power will affect the lives of the offenders in ways that are most uncomfortable. The text suggests that justice will be a corporate experience and not directed solely at the troublemakers. While God's actions here are depicted as less violent and destructive than they are elsewhere, God's wrath is not. The divine wrath and earthquake portrayed here may in fact, however, be symbolic.

Finally, the poet indicates that justice on behalf of the poor will eventually be served. Verses 7-8 feature God taking an oath, swearing never to forget any of the unethical deeds (8:7) and promising to chastise the mercenaries and barterers (8:8; see also 8:9-14).

9:1-10 Fifth vision: God

The theme of divine wrath continues in 9:1-10, the fifth of a series of vision reports in the book of Amos. In this passage Amos tells about a vision he had that concerns God's judgment upon the kingdom of Jeroboam.

Did I not bring the Israelites from
the land of Egypt
as I brought the Philistines from
Caphtor
and the Arameans from Kir?
⁸See, the eyes of the Lord GOD are
on this sinful kingdom,
and I will destroy it from the
face of the earth—
But I will not destroy the house of
Jacob completely—
oracle of the LORD.
⁹For see, I have given the command
to sift the house of Israel among
all the nations,
As one sifts with a sieve,
letting no pebble fall to the
ground.

¹⁰All sinners among my people
shall die by the sword,
those who say, "Disaster will
not reach or overtake us."

VI. Epilogue: Restoration Under a Davidic King

¹¹On that day I will raise up
the fallen hut of David;
I will wall up its breaches,
raise up its ruins,
and rebuild it as in the days of
old,
¹²That they may possess the
remnant of Edom,
and all nations claimed in my
name—

In this vision, the poet depicts God as one who authorizes power to be used destructively and promises to use it personally in the same way (9:1).

In verses 2-4 Amos describes God's inescapable wrath; the people will be made to suffer. God vows to snatch them from whatever hiding place they choose as an escape. If they dig into Sheol, God's hand will take them; if they climb up to heaven, God's hand will "bring them down" (9:2); if they hide on top of Carmel, God will search them out and take them; if they hide at the "bottom of the sea," God will "command the serpent to bite them" (9:3); if they "go into captivity before their enemies," God will "command the sword" and it shall kill them (9:4a). God's intentions are stated clearly in verse 4b.

Hence, God's sovereignty becomes an ominous and terrible reality, and God's punishment becomes an absolute finality. God has passed a legal verdict upon Israel for its transgressions, and judgment will be both punitive and intentional.

EPILOGUE

Amos 9:11-15

In Amos 9:11-15, the book's epilogue, a shift in tone occurs. In verses 11-12 Amos speaks of restoration and hope; in verses 13-15 he describes the coming of a new age. In metaphorical language, he announces the restoration

oracle of the LORD, the one who
does this.
¹³Yes, days are coming—
oracle of the LORD—
When the one who plows shall
overtake the one who reaps
and the vintager, the sower of
the seed;
The mountains shall drip with the
juice of grapes,
and all the hills shall run with it.
¹⁴I will restore my people Israel,

they shall rebuild and inhabit
their ruined cities,
Plant vineyards and drink the wine,
set out gardens and eat the
fruits.
¹⁵I will plant them upon their own
ground;
never again shall they be
plucked
From the land I have given them—
the LORD, your God, has spoken.

---

of the kingdom of David and Jerusalem, the place of David's reign (9:11). Verse 12 suggests that the restored kingdom's borders will extend to its fullest borders at the time of David. The nations that were part of the Davidic kingdom at its height were all promised to David and his descendants in God's name (2 Sam 7). Lastly, verses 13-15 promise a renewed covenant between God and the land, God and the people, and the people and the land.

Hosea

The book of Hosea is a complex and highly stylized text. Its backdrop is the rise of the Assyrian Empire in the mid-eighth century B.C. During this time period, Assyria became Israel's greatest threat. Little is known about Hosea, the book's prophet, who exposes Israel's apostasy, idolatry, and transgressions in vivid, metaphorical language that ranges from inferring that Israel is a prostitute (3:1-15) to calling Ephraim a trained heifer (10:11). Hosea's judgment on Israel is relentless (13:1-15), and Israel's transgressions are many (4:1-3). With great poignancy, Hosea captures the vacillation of God's heart as it struggles between bewilderment, remembrance, and sheer frustration only to let go to incredible compassion and understanding (11:1-9). True to his prophetic vocation, Hosea calls the people to repent (6:1-3; 14:1-3) and makes known to them that, indeed, God will heal their brokenness through transformative love (14:5-8). Like many of the other books of the prophets, Hosea closes on a note of hope. A people once forsaken will now become God's own again, living in God's shade and "blossom[ing] like the vine" (14:8).

The historical and social world of Hosea

Interestingly, the book of Hosea does not portray the actual Assyrian invasions of Israel. The text was written, for the most part, in the period following the death of Jeroboam II and just prior to the Assyrian assault in 735–732 B.C. The purpose of this setting was to convince Israel to abandon its alliance with Assyria. Furthermore, Hosea seemed to have been in debate over Israel's future from the end of the Jehu dynasty to the emergence of Pekah, who was eventually assassinated by Hoshea during the Assyrians' invasion of Israel.

Like the world of Amos, a contemporary of Hosea, Hosea's world was fraught with idolatry, apostasy, and transgressions. Hosea's primary focus was on the religious state of affairs of Israel and Judah. He condemned Baal worship (2:10, 15, 18, 19; 9:10; 13:1), which also included cultic rites on the high places (4:13; 10:8), pillars (3:4; 10:1-2), divining rods (4:12), images (4:17; 8:4; 14:9), and calf figurines (8:5-6; 10:5; 13:2). All of these elements had, at one time, been part of early Israelite religion and the worship of God. Hosea seems

to have been condemning early Yahwism. Like Amos, Hosea dealt with the poverty and injustice of his day, both of which flowed from a time of prosperity and grandeur. Finally, although the text may have been written after the death of Jeroboam II, the text itself seems to reflect the last years of Jeroboam II's reign. Pinpointing actual historical referents within the book, however, is difficult because many of the proclamations are obscure and allusive.

The literary dimensions of the book of Hosea

Perhaps the most striking literary aspect of the book of Hosea is its metaphorical language, with many of the images coming from the natural world and reflective of agriculture and husbandry. God is described as a physician (7:1; 14:5), a shepherd (13:5), and a fowler (7:12). God is also said to be like the dawn (6:3a), spring rains (6:3b), a lion (13:7a), a leopard (13:7b), a bear (13:8), dew (14:6), and an evergreen cypress (14:9). Israel is like a dove (7:11; cf. 9:11), a luxurious vine (10:1), morning cloud (13:3a), dew (13:3b), and chaff (13:3). Hosea 1–3 features an extended metaphor: the infidelity of Gomer mirrors the infidelity of Israel. Hosea 10:1 is another extended metaphor. The book also features warfare imagery that foreshadows impending disaster for Judah (5:8-14; 8:1). Contrasting the warfare imagery is the tender maternal/paternal imagery of a God who remembers caring for Israel as a child (11:1-4) with a heart that now vacillates between anger and compassion (11:9). In the midst of the book's many judgment proclamations are heartfelt pleas for repentance (14:2-3) and promises of healing and renewal (14:5-9). Thus, the style and tone of the book of Hosea shift back and forth from threat to consolation, from frustration to compassion, from impatience to understanding on God's part.

With respect to structure, the book is comprised of two main parts: Hosea's marriage (1–3) and Hosea's prophecies (4–14). The text can be further divided into the following units:

I. Superscription (1:1)
II. Marriage metaphor; Gomer, Hosea, God, and Israel (1:2–3:5)
    First judgment speech against Israel (1:2-9)
    Word of promise and hope (2:1-3)
    Second judgment speech against Israel (2:4-25)
    Symbolic action and word of hope (3:1-5)
III. Proclamation against Israel and its leadership (4:1–5:7)
    Address to the people of Israel (4:1-3)
    Address to Israel's priests (4:4-19)
    Address to Israel's priests, kings, and people (5:1-7)

The prophet Hosea, sculpted by Aleijadinho, in front of the church of the Sanctuary of Bom Jesus of Matosinhos at Congonhas, Minas Gerais, Brazil.

Even though the metaphorical language and imagery add color to the text of Hosea, this language and imagery do raise points for further hermeneutical consideration. For example, some of the gender-specific metaphors can be deemed offensive to women. A clear example is the extended marriage metaphor in Hosea 1–3, where the relationship between Hosea and Gomer is supposed to represent the relationship between God and Israel. Hosea and God, the male figures in the text, are the faithful ones; Gomer and Israel, the female figures, are the unfaithful ones. The imagery is difficult because the culture of the day privileged males. Additionally, Gomer remains voiceless in the text. Her experience in the marriage remains unheard. Often in the ancient world, particularly during monarchal times, women were looked upon as subordinate to men.

Furthermore, those metaphors that compare people to animals and plant life deserve further thought and comment. Unless people understand life on the planet as a non-hierarchical relationship among all life forms—truly the interdependence of all life in the web of life—then those metaphors that compare people to animals and plant life can be looked upon as diminution. Finally, the war imagery in the text also reflects the culture of the day and continues to influence readers' political and theological imagination at a time when new paradigms of justice are sorely needed in the search for peace.

The theological dimensions of the book of Hosea

Like his eighth-century-B.C. contemporaries, specifically First Isaiah, Amos, and Micah, the prophet Hosea paints a larger-than-life portrait of God to assert divine authority and sovereignty over all peoples and all gods throughout the entire region. The primary focus of the prophet's message is, however, that God is God of Israel, and Israel is God's people. Covenant love is central to the book. This covenant love entails a bond in love and a strong trustworthiness. The book of Hosea is the first prophetic text to envision covenant love as a marriage, and while the metaphor is effective and lends a personal and intimate dimension to the legal framework of the Mosaic covenant, the metaphor also has its limitations, as noted earlier.

In addition to the focus on divine sovereignty and covenant relationship, the book of Hosea has as its theological fabric a series of blessings and curses reflective of the Mosaic law. Thus, the relationship between covenant and law is paramount in the text and central to the prophet's proclamations. Perhaps the most important theological point that can be gleaned from the book as a whole is Hosea 11:9:

> For I am God and not a man,
> the Holy One present among you;
> I will not come in wrath.

Israel's God, though depicted in anthropomorphic, anthropocentric, and androcentric ways, truly is not a human being and does not resolve issues as human beings would and did in the eighth century B.C. Thus, the image of Israel's God as warrior and a fire-and-brimstone God is the product of religious imagination used by the biblical poets to make a specific point in each of the Bible's Prophetic Books. Perhaps the greatest and most accurate quality humans can ascribe to God who is Sacred Mystery is compassion (14:3), which, for believers then and now, is a metaphor that flows from lived experience instead of metaphors that come from having read God and God's ways into life's inevitable events.

Finally, the book of Hosea holds out hope not only for those who are victims of injustice but also for those who cause the injustice. Perpetrators of wickedness and transgressors of covenant and torah are beckoned to return to God (14:2) to meet the face of compassion (14:4) and to experience the profound touch of healing (14:5-8). Thus, the theological message of the book of Hosea is timeless and remains inviting.

Hosea

◄ 1 ¹The word of the Lord that came to Hosea son of Beeri, in the days of Uzziah, Jotham, Ahaz, Hezekiah, kings of Judah, and in the days of Jeroboam, son of Joash, king of Israel.

I. The Prophet's Marriage and its Symbolism

Marriage of Hosea and Gomer. ²When the Lord began to speak with Hosea, the Lord said to Hosea: Go, get for yourself a woman of prostitution and children of prostitution, for the land prostitutes itself, turning away from the Lord.

³So he went and took Gomer, daughter of Diblaim; and she conceived and bore him a son. ⁴Then the Lord said to him: Give him the name "Jezreel," for in a little while I will punish the house of Jehu for the bloodshed at Jezreel and

SUPERSCRIPTION

Hosea 1:1

The book of Hosea opens with a superscription typical of other prophetic books (see, e.g., Isa 1:1; Jer 1:1-3; Amos 1:1; Mic 1:1; Zeph 1:1). This superscription names Hosea's father and situates Hosea's ministry in the mid-eighth century B.C., which was marked by the rise of the Assyrian Empire and the threat it posed to the northern kingdom Israel. According to the list of kings presented in the superscription, Hosea is said to have preached during the reigns of four Judean kings—Uzziah, 783–742 B.C.; Jotham, 742–735 B.C.; Ahaz, 735–715 B.C.; and Hezekiah, 715–687 B.C.—and one Israelite king, Jeroboam II (786–746 B.C.). Supposedly, Hosea's ministry began toward the end of the reign of Jeroboam II. Oddly, only one Israelite king is mentioned, which may, in part, be due to the chaos occurring in the northern kingdom after his reign or, since all the Prophetic Books were edited and passed on in Judah, the listing may reflect a Judean bias in the text. The Israelite northern kingdom was destroyed in 721/722 B.C. Hosea repeatedly warns the inhabitants of Israel about the terror that is about to befall them and pleads with them to restore their covenant relationship with God. Kings not mentioned included Zechariah, Shallum, Menahem,

bring to an end the kingdom of the house of Israel; ⁵on that day I will break the bow of Israel in the valley of Jezreel.

⁶She conceived again and bore a daughter. The LORD said to him: Give her the name "Not-Pitied," for I will no longer feel pity for the house of Israel:

rather, I will utterly abhor them. ⁷Yet for the house of Judah I will feel pity; I will save them by the LORD, their God; but I will not save them by bow or sword, by warfare, by horses or horsemen.

⁸After she weaned Not-Pitied, she conceived and bore a son. ⁹Then the

Pekahiah, Pekah, and Hoshea. Only two of them—Menahem and Hoshea—were not assassinated by their successors.

MARRIAGE METAPHOR; GOMER, HOSEA, GOD, AND ISRAEL

Hosea 1:2–3:5

This first major unit of the book of Hosea is couched in metaphorical language and images that describe God's fidelity to the Israelite people despite their infidelities to God, to covenant, and to torah. The poet reminds Hosea's listeners then and now that judgment is never the final word. Hope remains central to the fabric of life and to the prophetic tradition as a whole.

1:2-9 First judgment speech against Israel

Hosea 1:2-9 is the first judgment speech against Israel. In verse 2 the marriage metaphor used to express the relationship between Hosea and Gomer is first introduced, and it represents the marriage between God and Israel. Just as Hosea is to take a wife of prostitution, so God will take back idolatrous, apostate, unfaithful Israel, who has "played the whore" by turning to other gods and trusting in alliances instead of relying on God and focusing on God's ways, covenant, and law.

With respect to the issue of prostitution, within the ancient world this form of conduct was not altogether a lack of moral character but rather a matter of economic necessity if women lacked financial support in the patriarchal social structure in which they found themselves. This structure made women dependent upon male relatives—a father, a husband, a brother, a son, or a next of kin male—for property rights and the produce of the land. If no support was given, then she had to find a way to support herself outside of the normal structure. Quite possibly Gomer may not have been a woman of poor character but rather a woman who had to turn to harlotry in order to support herself. Furthermore, the reference to "children of prostitution" (1:2) does not imply that the children were not Hosea's offspring after he married Gomer. The phrase is merely one that signifies the status of their mother.

LORD said: Give him the name "Not-My-People," for you are not my people, and I am not "I am" for you.

2 ¹The number of the Israelites
will be like the sand of the sea,
which can be neither measured
nor counted.

Instead of being told,
"You are Not-My-People,"
They will be called,
"Children of the living God."
²Then the people of Judah and of
Israel
will gather together;

In verse 3 the biblical writer features Hosea carrying out God's command without any dialogue or second thought. This verse bolsters the intent of the book as a whole, which is meant to persuade its audience to change its ways so as to avert the disaster and so-called "divine punishment" announced throughout the book. Hosea takes Gomer as his wife; they have relations; she bears him a son, whom he is to name "Jezreel" (1:4), a symbolic appellation of past and future events. "Jezreel" means "God plants" or "God sows." The history behind Jezreel, a place, is rich. Jezreel was a beautiful valley located strategically between the mountains of Galilee and Samaria. There the Jehu dynasty began with the bloody overthrow of the house of Omri. Second Kings 9–10 records the past events that resulted in the assassination of King Joram of Israel, Joram's cousin King Ahaziah ben Jehoshaphat of Judah, and also Jezebel, Joram's mother. After these events, seventy sons of Ahab were killed in Jezreel by the supporters of Jehu, the ancestor of Jeroboam ben Joash (1:1). Jehu is presented in 2 Kings 10:28-31 as someone who did not observe God's commandments. He did, however, destroy the supporters of Baal and consequently eliminated the Omride dynasty and all its supporters. Omri, Ahab, and Jezebel were considered to be evil leaders because they led the people away from God and God's ways. Thus, verses 3-5 foreshadow two points: Jezreel will be avenged and the northern kingdom Israel will be destroyed. The name Jezreel appears later in Hosea where the defeated Jezreel turns into a word of restoration and a new beginning.

Verse 6 describes the daughter born to Gomer and Hosea. Like her brother Jezreel, she too has a symbolic name and function. Gomer and Hosea's daughter is to be named *lo-ruhamah*, "Not-Pitied." God is no longer going to show mercy on the house of Israel, which is a clear reversal of the relationship between God and Israel as laid out in the Mosaic law and tradition. God's love and mercy were foundational to Israel's self-understanding and self-identity.

God, however, has not turned away from the people completely. Judah will experience God's compassion and will be saved by God (1:7). This statement is curious, though, because Judah is eventually destroyed by the

They will appoint for themselves
    one head
    and rise up from the land;
    great indeed shall be the day of
      Jezreel!
³Say to your brothers, "My People,"
    and to your sisters, "Pitied."

The Lord and Israel His Spouse

⁴Accuse your mother, accuse!
    for she is not my wife,

and I am not her husband.
Let her remove her prostitution
    from her face.
    her adultery from between her
      breasts,
⁵Or I will strip her naked,
    leaving her as on the day of her
      birth;
I will make her like the wilderness,
    make her like an arid land,
    and let her die of thirst.

Babylonians. The reference could be to the Assyrian invasion led by Sennacherib in 701 B.C. (see 2 Kgs 19:32-37), a time when Jerusalem somehow escaped destruction. The phrase could also have been added into the book before the fall of the southern kingdom of Judah in 587 B.C.

Verses 8-9 describe a third child born to Gomer and Hosea. This child, a son, is to be named *lo-ammi*, "Not-My-People." This name signifies the end of God's covenantal relationship with the people. The phrase "my people" was often used to describe God's covenant with Israel (see, e.g., Exod 6:7; Lev 26:12; Deut 26:17-19; 2 Sam 7:24; Jer 11:4). Thus, the biblical writer portrays God as being thoroughly disgusted with the Israelites.

2:1-3 Word of promise and hope

Hosea 2:1-3 shifts from judgment to promise and hope. Israel's time of chastisement and lamentation will not last forever. Israel's God, although enraged by the people's idolatry, apostasy, and waywardness, will not break covenant. The metaphorical language that describes the number of Israelites in relation to the sand of the sea that can neither be measured nor counted recalls the ancient promises spoken to Abraham and Jacob (see, e.g., Gen 13:16; 22:17; 26:24; 28:13-14).

Finally, Israel and God's estrangement from each other will be reversed. Eventually a new kingdom will emerge, one that combines both the northern kingdom of Israel and the southern kingdom of Judah. Covenant renewal will take place, signified by the reversal of the children's names.

2:4-25 Second judgment speech against Israel

Hosea 2:4-25 is part of a larger unit, chapters 1–3, that focuses on the husband-wife metaphor. The setting for this passage is Hosea's bitter marital experience with Gomer, his promiscuous wife. Like Gomer, Israel has been unfaithful to God, going after and worshiping Canaanite deities and thus breaking covenant.

⁶I will have no pity on her children,
    for they are children of
        prostitution.
⁷Yes, their mother has prostituted
    herself;
    she who conceived them has
        acted shamefully.
For she said, "I will go after my
    lovers,
    who give me my bread and my
        water,
    my wool and my flax, my oil
        and my drink."
⁸Therefore, I will hedge in her way
    with thorns
    and erect a wall against her,
    so that she cannot find her paths.

⁹If she runs after her lovers, she will
    not overtake them;
    if she seeks them she will not
        find them.
Then she will say,
    "I will go back to my first
        husband,
    for I was better off then than
        now."
¹⁰She did not know
    that it was I who gave her
    the grain, the wine, and the oil,
I who lavished upon her silver,
    and gold, which they used for
        Baal,
¹¹Therefore I will take back my
    grain in its time,

In verses 4-5 Hosea makes a passionate plea to his children to have them confront their mother about her adulterous ways. Hosea wants Gomer to end her harlotry. The punch line, however, comes in verse 5, where Hosea issues a threat. Either she stops her whoring or he will strip her naked, expose her, make her a wilderness, turn her into a parched land, and kill her with thirst. On one level, these two verses apply to Gomer; on another level, these verses symbolically speak about God's relationship with Israel—Israel's infidelity and what God plans to do to Israel if she does not refrain from her whoring, her idolatrous ways.

Verse 6 continues the series of threats begun in verses 4-5. Hosea/God states that no pity will be given to Gomer's/Israel's children because they are children of prostitution (2:6). Verse 7 expands on verse 4. Hosea/God describes in detail Gomer's/Israel's infidelities.

Verses 8-15 state a series of punishments that husband Hosea/God will inflict on wife Gomer/Israel. Gomer/Israel stands accused of fickleness in infidelity, and ignorance, for she did not know that it was her husband who had given her all sorts of gifts that were later used for Baal (2:10). Perhaps the most graphic and most brutal expression of punishment appears in verses 11-15, where Hosea/God declares that he will (1) take back his grain, wine, and oil, along with his wool and flax that were used to cover her nakedness; (2) uncover her shame in the sight of all her lovers; (3) allow no one to rescue her from his hand; (4) put an end to all her festivals; (5) "lay waste her vines and fig trees"; and (6) punish her for her apostate ways and forgetfulness of Hosea/God.

and my wine in its season;
I will snatch away my wool and my
flax,
which were to cover her
nakedness.
¹²Now I will lay bare her shame
in full view of her lovers,
and no one can deliver her out
of my hand.
¹³I will put an end to all her joy,
her festivals, her new moons,
her sabbaths—

all her seasonal feasts.
¹⁴I will lay waste her vines and fig
trees,
of which she said, "These are
the fees
my lovers have given me";
I will turn them into rank growth
and wild animals shall devour
them.
¹⁵I will punish her for the days of
the Baals,
for whom she burnt incense,

Following a lengthy judgment speech (2:4-15), Hosea 2:16-17 initiates a shift in tone and images. Having been presented with a picture of an angry God enraged with Israel, expressed through the metaphorical language and imagery of a husband-wife relationship, the section portrays a God who woos Israel with tender words and the promise of a renewed relationship with the land and with God (2:16). After all of the harsh punishments that Gomer/Israel will have to endure, Hosea/God then promises to allure Gomer/Israel into the wilderness so that he can speak tenderly to her, give her vineyards, and thus win her back to himself, with her responding to him as she did in the days of her youth (2:16-17). Thus, in verses 16-17 the poet envisions Israel's turn from apostasy to faithfulness, a turn that God initiates.

Looking at verses 4-17 as a whole, we see that the poet has depicted Hosea/God as an enraged husband whose anger leads to several threats that are punitive and violent emotionally, physically, and psychologically for wife Gomer/Israel, who is to be mercilessly exposed to all "her" lovers. She will then be made to suffer serious consequences for "her" infidelity, only to be wooed again by her husband, whose anger has been expressed abusively. Contemporary believers and readers are faced with a series of ethical and theological considerations, generated first by the initial understanding of covenant as a marital relationship, and second by the gender-specific metaphorical language that brings the marital notion of covenant to life. The question becomes, then, "How humanly and divinely ethical is Hosea's message, which bespeaks of violence being used as a corrective for violence, and how appropriate is this metaphor for today when speaking about covenant and relationships?"

One can conclude that the metaphorical language in Hosea 2:4-17 calls for a reappropriation of the prophet's message in light of contemporary life experiences that reflect situations of violence and abuse, inclusive of marital

When she decked herself out with
    her rings and her jewelry,
and went after her lovers—
    but me she forgot—oracle of the
      LORD.
¹⁶Therefore, I will allure her now;
    I will lead her into the wilderness
and speak persuasively to her.
¹⁷Then I will give her the vineyards
    she had,
and the valley of Achor as a
      door of hope.
There she will respond as in the
    days of her youth,

as on the day when she came up
    from the land of Egypt.

¹⁸On that day—oracle of the LORD—
You shall call me "My husband,"
    and you shall never again call
      me "My baal."
¹⁹I will remove from her mouth the
    names of the Baals;
they shall no longer be
      mentioned by their name.

²⁰I will make a covenant for them
    on that day,
with the wild animals,

---

infidelities and discords that have ended violently. Even though the language of the passage may reflect the social setting and cultural perspectives of its day, such language has the potential to negatively affect one's theological imagination as well as one's understanding of and relationship with God and with other human beings. Thus, Hosea 2:4-17 inspires further ethical and hermeneutical reflection and invites the creation of new metaphors that call people to an abiding sense of respect and integrity in all relationships, even in the face of human frailty and infidelity.

One of the central themes of the Old Testament is covenant. God enters into a covenant with Noah, Abraham, Moses and the Israelites at Sinai, and David, and promises a new covenant to Jeremiah and Hosea. Like the Noahic covenant, the covenant promised in Hosea involves God, people, and the natural world. With this covenant the poet envisions a time when God will restore the land to Israel. God promises to make for the Israelites a covenant "with the wild animals, / With the birds of the air, / and with the things that crawl on the ground" (2:20). This covenant is similar to the covenant that God made with Noah, Noah's descendants, and with every living creature that was with Noah (Gen 9:10). Although the Hosea covenant uses espousal imagery that can be disconcerting for reasons mentioned earlier (see 2:4-17), this new covenant envisions harmonious relationships that flow from the relationship with God. For the people of Hosea's time, this covenant offered tremendous hope.

Verse 20, which is, perhaps, the heart of the pericope, depicts a renewed relationship between human beings and the natural world and an end to violence. Peace and security for all creation (2:20) are intricately linked to the renewal of relationship between God and human beings (2:21-22).

With the birds of the air,
and with the things that crawl
on the ground.
Bow and sword and warfare
I will destroy from the land,
and I will give them rest in
safety.

◄ ²¹I will betroth you to me forever:
I will betroth you to me with
justice and with judg-
ment,
with loyalty and with
compassion;
²²I will betroth you to me with
fidelity,

and you shall know the LORD.
²³On that day I will respond—
oracle of the LORD—
I will respond to the heavens,
and they will respond to the
earth;
²⁴The earth will respond to the
grain, and wine, and oil,
and these will respond to Jezreel.
²⁵I will sow her for myself in the
land,
and I will have pity on Not-
Pitied.
I will say to Not-My-People, "You
are my people,"
and he will say, "My God!"

Through the redemption and restoration of the Israelite people to their God, the natural world is also redeemed and restored.

Verses 23-25 open with a stock phrase, "On that day" (2:23). The future holds a day of divine blessing and a time of cosmic salvation: heaven and earth will now answer each other, and the earth shall respond to its productivity, which, in turn, will respond to human beings as symbolized by the name of Hosea's child Jezreel, which means "God plants." Finally, God will respond to Hosea's children, that is, the covenant people, in the land. Furthermore, in these verses the poet allows us to see that God will re-establish the divine activities that unite both the natural world and humankind.

Thus, in Hosea 2:20-25, the poet presents a visionary picture that speaks of a new covenant that will affect all creation. The passage depicts a new understanding of the relationship between human beings and the natural world, one that is mutual and interdependent, affirming that the redemption of humanity is connected with the restoration of creation. This divinely promised redemption and restoration leads to a vision of creation that embodies justice, righteousness, peace, and harmonious relationships. Finally, from a hermeneutical perspective, Hosea 2:20-25 challenges contemporary readers to a new ethic, a justice that is not anthropocentric in nature and construct but, rather, one that speaks of justice for all creation. The biblical vision of covenant in Hosea is cosmic and carries with it the potential for a new global ethic.

Hosea and His Wife Reunited

3 ¹Again the Lᴏʀᴅ said to me:

Go, love a woman
   who is loved by her spouse but
      commits adultery;
Just as the Lᴏʀᴅ loves the Israelites,
   though they turn to other gods
   and love raisin cakes.

²So I acquired her for myself for fifteen pieces of silver and a homer and a lethech of barley. ³Then I said to her:

"You will wait for me for many
      days;
   you will not prostitute yourself
Or belong to any man;
   I in turn will wait for you."
⁴For the Israelites will remain many
      days
   without king or prince,
Without sacrifice or sacred pillar,
   without ephod or household
      gods.
⁵Afterward the Israelites will turn
      back
   and seek the Lᴏʀᴅ, their God,
   and David, their king;
They will come trembling to the
      Lᴏʀᴅ
   and to his bounty, in the last
      days.

3:1-5 Symbolic action and word of hope

Hosea 3:1-5 returns to the story of Hosea, and God's desire that Hosea love a woman. In verse 1 the poet depicts God issuing a command to Hosea, telling him a second time to go and love a woman guilty of adultery. The woman is unnamed. She may or may not be Gomer. Most likely, the woman is not Gomer, contrary to popular scholarly thought. The text makes no mention of Gomer being unfaithful to Hosea in 1:1–2:25. There Gomer is described as a woman of prostitution or harlotry. Here this woman is described as an adulterous woman. Thus, this woman mentioned in verse 1 seems to be a different one from Gomer.

In verses 2-5 Hosea complies with God's request and then issues a command to the woman. She is not to practice harlotry nor is she to be with Hosea either. Again, Hosea's actions become an analogy for God's relationship with Israel. A period of separation is to occur that will spark a contrite state on the part of the people. This separation from God will have profound ramifications for Israel. The people will have no king or prince, hence, no government of their own and no public manifestation of worship. This time of separation will be an experience of purification for Israel and, eventually, it will lead to restoration and renewal with a new king—one like David— promised to the people.

Thus, Hosea 1:2–3:5 is highly metaphorical and describes God's agony, disappointment, and rage over Israel's sordid state. Israel's God, however, never abandons covenant. Despite all of the people's failings, God remains faithful to them, even though the relationship may be strained for a while.

II. Israel's Guilt, Punishment, and Restoration

4 **Indictment of Israel.** ¹Hear the word of the LORD, Israelites,
   for the LORD has a dispute
      with the inhabitants of the land:
   There is no fidelity, no loyalty,
      no knowledge of God in the
         land.
²Swearing, lying, murder,
   stealing and adultery break out;
   bloodshed follows bloodshed.
³Therefore the land dries up,
   and everything that dwells in it
      languishes:
The beasts of the field,
   the birds of the air,
   and even the fish of the sea
      perish.

Guilt of Priest and of People
⁴But let no one accuse, let no one
   rebuke;
   with you is my dispute, priest!
⁵You will stumble in the day,
   and the prophet will stumble
      with you at night;
   I will make an end of your
      mother.
⁶My people are ruined for lack of
   knowledge!

PROCLAMATION AGAINST ISRAEL AND ITS LEADERSHIP

Hosea 4:1–5:7

4:1-3 Address to the people of Israel

The prophet Hosea speaks of the suffering of the land in relation to human sinfulness. The most striking passage is Hosea 4:1-3, a judgment speech (a *rib*) against Israel. In verses 1-2 Hosea outlines the grievances that Yahweh has against Israel: lack of fidelity and loyalty, no knowledge of God in the land, swearing, lying, murder, stealing, adultery, and continuous bloodshed. The conjunction "Therefore" in verse 3 begins the description of the land's suffering. Implied is that the suffering will be the result of divine judgment that will take the form of a drought. Hosea draws a connection between the suffering of the land and human sinfulness. Not only is the land affected but also the animals and fish, which, like the land, have done nothing to deserve such painful chastisement. By causing the land to experience a drought, God causes the people to suffer: the land will not be able to produce food or sustain any wildlife, and hence the people will have no food and eventually die. In the ancient world, the people believed that droughts and the like were caused by God and were the effects of divine chastisement for sin.

4:4-19 Address to Israel's priests

Hosea also exposes the complacency of Israel's religious leaders. Following his enumeration of Israel's transgressions (4:1-3), he indicts those priests of his day (4:4-13), while mentioning the prophets (4:5), who have

Since you have rejected knowledge,
I will reject you from serving as
my priest;
Since you have forgotten the law of
your God,
I will also forget your children.

⁷The more they multiplied, the
more they sinned against me,
I will change their glory into
shame.
⁸They feed on the sin of my people,
and are greedy for their iniquity.
⁹Like people, like priest:
I will punish them for their
ways,
and repay them for their deeds.
¹⁰They will eat but not be satisfied,
they will promote prostitution
but not increase,
Because they have abandoned the
LORD,
devoting themselves
¹¹to prostitution.
Aged wine and new wine
take away understanding.
¹²My people consult their piece of
wood,
and their wand makes
pronouncements for
them,
For the spirit of prostitution has led
them astray;

---

neglected their responsibilities to the detriment of the Israelite community. Part of a longer accusation (4:1-13), verses 4-13 describe God's contention with the priests: they have rejected knowledge and forgotten the law of their God. Consequently, the people are "ruined for lack of knowledge" (4:6). Furthermore, the priests are profiting personally from the people's transgressions since they receive a certain portion of the atonement offerings that the guilty ones would bring to the sanctuaries (4:8).

God's response to the priests' infidelities and deplorable deeds is candid and without compassion. Hosea declares that God will destroy their mothers (4:5), reject them as priests (4:6), forget their children (4:6), "punish them for their ways" (4:9), "repay them for their deeds" (4:9), and allow them to experience no personal satisfaction from their gain or deeds (4:10). Without a doubt, certain religious leaders—here, the priest—have corrupted their office and neglected their responsibilities. For Hosea, the behavior of the priest(s) becomes an ethical issue. Corruption within the priesthood does not go unnoticed by Hosea and, according to the prophet, will not go unchecked by God.

Hosea 4:12-14 describes the actions of the people. They are guilty of consulting pieces of wood and having their wands "make pronouncements for them" (4:12a). The pieces of wood could be a reference to the Canaanite fertility goddess Asherah, but more probably the reference is to the Levitical rod or staff that the Levites and priests carried to symbolize their status. Through the use of such imagery, the poet makes the point that the priesthood is ineffective. Furthermore, the people sacrifice and burn incense on

they prostitute themselves,
    forsaking their God.
[13]On the mountaintops they offer
    sacrifice
and on the hills they burn
    incense,
Beneath oak and poplar and
    terebinth,
because of their pleasant shade.
Therefore your daughters prostitute
    themselves,
    and your daughters-in-law
        commit adultery.
[14]I will not punish your daughters
    for their prostitution,

nor your daughters-in-law for
    their adultery,
Because the men themselves con-
    sort with prostitutes,
and with temple women they
    offer sacrifice!
Thus a people without under-
    standing comes to ruin.

[15]Though you prostitute yourself,
    Israel,
    do not let Judah become guilty!
Do not come to Gilgal,
    do not go up to Beth-aven,
    do not swear, "As the Lord lives!"

---

the mountaintops and hills. Thus, the people are guilty of apostasy and probably even pagan worship outside of God's temple (see, e.g., Deut 12:2; 1 Kgs 14:23; Isa 65:7; Jer 2:20; Ezek 18:6, 11, 15 for similar imagery), and because of such a sordid religious state, the people fall into a sordid social state (4:13). All of their actions reap divine judgment (4:14). In sum, the priests were responsible for educating the people in the torah but their failure to do so has led the people into apostasy (here, expressed as prostitution and adultery) and caused them God's wrath.

Words of reproach directed toward the Israelites continue in Hosea 4:15-19. These verses continue themes heard earlier in verses 11-14: whoredom (4:11, 15), drunkenness (4:11, 18), and idolatry (4:13, 17). The mention of Judah in verse 15 is curious. Even though Hosea was a prophet who spoke to the northern kingdom, the book itself is addressed to the southern kingdom Judah in the aftermath of the destruction of the northern kingdom Israel. Finally, Hosea sees Israel as being stubborn (4:16); the kingdom of Israel is joined to idols (4:17); worship has become a mockery (4:18); the people have been caught up by a strange wind, otherwise known as idolatry, and they will suffer consequences (4:19). Thus, the people's lack of knowledge and understanding (4:6, 14) and the corruption of their religious leaders, whose responsibility is to instruct the Israelites in torah, will have severe implications.

To contemporary readers Hosea 4:4-19 suggests that in ancient Israel problems existed within the cult that demanded an ethical response from those prophets who, like Hosea, speak out because of their fidelity to God and the ensuing responsibilities that such a commitment brings. Hosea's

¹⁶For like a stubborn cow,
Israel is stubborn;
Will the LORD now pasture them,
like lambs in a broad meadow?
¹⁷Ephraim is bound to idols,
let him alone!
¹⁸When their drinking is over,
they give themselves to
prostitution;
they love shame more than their
honor.
¹⁹A wind has bound them up in its
wings;
they shall be ashamed because
of their altars.

Guilt of the Religious and Political Leaders

5 ¹Hear this, priests,
Pay attention, house of Israel,
Household of the king, give ear!
For you are responsible for
judgment.
But you have been a snare at
Mizpah,
a net spread upon Tabor,
²a pit dug deep in Shittim.
Now I will discipline them all.

³I know Ephraim,
and Israel is not hidden from me:

---

ethical response, however, invites continued ethical and theological reflection, particularly with respect to the comment that the priest's mother would be destroyed and the children forgotten (see 4:5, 6). While such metaphorical language intensifies the prophet's message and might even strike the heart of the accused, such language raises a problem: Should others be made to suffer as a chastisement for another's transgression, as the text suggests? Even if the language is metaphorical, it communicates an attitude that sanctions justice at the expense of the society's least powerful and the most vulnerable—women and children.

5:1-7 Address to Israel's priests, kings, and people

Hosea 5:1-7, an address to Israel's religious and political leaders, develops the imagery of Hosea's marriage to Gomer heard earlier in Hosea 1–2. Once again, Israel stands condemned (5:1-2). Israel's deeds (5:3), duplicitous heart and spirit (5:4), and unbridled arrogance (5:5) condemned here are the alliances Israel made with Assyria and Egypt (see 5:13-14; 7:11-12). Israel's inability to see the relationship that needs to exist between worship and how the people live their lives on a daily basis becomes evident in verses 6-7. In these verses the poet portrays the people coming with their flocks and cattle to seek God. Israel's God, however, withdraws from them on account of their betrayal. Significant here is the fact that God does not abandon the people; God "withdraws" from them. To abandon them would be to break covenant, which would go against the promises made to Abraham and Israel's ancestors down through the ages. As the poet reiterates again and again throughout the book of Hosea, God remains faithful to covenant despite the people's infidelity.

Now, Ephraim, you have practiced
    prostitution,
    Israel is defiled.
⁴Their deeds do not allow them
    to return to their God;
For the spirit of prostitution is in
    them,
    and they do not know the LORD.

⁵The arrogance of Israel bears
    witness against him;
    Israel and Ephraim stumble
        because of their iniquity,
    and Judah stumbles with them.
⁶With their flocks and herds they
    will go
    to seek the LORD, but will not
        find him;
    he has withdrawn from them.
⁷They have betrayed the LORD,
    for they have borne illegitimate
        children;
Now the new moon will devour
    them
    together with their fields.

Political Upheavals

⁸Blow the ram's horn in Gibeah,
    the trumpet in Ramah!

Sound the alarm in Beth-aven:
    "Look behind you, Benjamin!"
⁹Ephraim shall become a wasteland
    on the day of punishment:
Among the tribes of Israel
    I announce what is sure to be.
¹⁰The princes of Judah have become
    like those who move a boundary
        line;
Upon them I will pour out
    my wrath like water.
¹¹Ephraim is oppressed, crushed by
    judgment,
    for he has willingly gone after
        filth!
¹²I am like a moth for Ephraim,
    like rot for the house of Judah.
¹³When Ephraim saw his infirmity,
    and Judah his sore,
Ephraim went to Assyria,
    and sent to the great king.
But he cannot heal you,
    nor take away your sore.
¹⁴For I am like a lion to Ephraim,
    like a young lion to the house of
        Judah;
It is I who tear the prey and depart,
    I carry it away and no one can
        save it.

JUDGMENT SPEECH AGAINST ISRAEL AND JUDAH

Hosea 5:8-14

In this next unit, Hosea 5:8-14, the focus shifts from idolatry to war (5:8). Israel and Judah must now prepare to do battle with God, who will be "like a lion to Ephraim" and "a young lion to the house of Judah" (5:14). These verses foreshadow the demise of the northern kingdom Israel and the southern kingdom Judah by the Assyrians and the Babylonians, respectively. Israel's lack of trust in God, signified by the alliances made with Assyria (5:13), is a sharp bone of contention with God, who points out the folly of such a choice (5:13-14) that will have consequences (5:9, 11, 13).

Insincere Conversion

¹⁵I will go back to my place
    until they make reparation
    and seek my presence.
In their affliction, they shall look for
    me.

6 ¹"Come, let us return to the Lord,
For it is he who has torn, but he
    will heal us;
    he has struck down, but he will
        bind our wounds.
²He will revive us after two days;
    on the third day he will raise us
        up,
    to live in his presence.
³Let us know, let us strive to know
    the Lord;
    as certain as the dawn is his
        coming.
He will come to us like the rain,
    like spring rain that waters the
        earth."

⁴What can I do with you, Ephraim?
    What can I do with you, Judah?
Your loyalty is like morning mist,
    like the dew that disappears
        early.
⁵For this reason I struck them down
    through the prophets,
    I killed them by the words of
        my mouth;
    my judgment shines forth like
        the light.
⁶For it is loyalty that I desire, not
    sacrifice,
and knowledge of God rather
    than burnt offerings.

Further Crimes of Israel

⁷But they, at Adam, violated the
    covenant;
    there they betrayed me.

⁸Gilead is a city of evildoers,
    tracked with blood.
⁹Like brigands lying in wait
    is the band of priests.
They murder on the road to
    Shechem,
    indeed they commit a monstrous
        crime.
¹⁰In the house of Israel I have seen a
    horrible thing:
    there is found Ephraim's
        prostitution,
    Israel is defiled.
¹¹For you also, Judah,
    a harvest has been appointed!

7 When I would have restored the fortunes of my people,
¹when I would have healed
    Israel,
The guilt of Ephraim was revealed,
    the wickedness of Samaria:
    They practiced falsehood.
Thieves break in,
    bandits roam outside.
²Yet they do not call to mind
    that I remember all their
        wickedness.
Now their crimes surround them,
    present to my sight.

EXPRESSION OF DIVINE FRUSTRATION AND JUDGMENT UPON ISRAEL AND JUDAH

Hosea 5:15–7:2

In this next section, the poet portrays Israel's God as being not only disgruntled (5:15) but also frustrated (6:4–7:2) by an untrusting, unfaithful people despite Hosea's words of encouragement (6:1-3).

Hosea 5:15–7:2 opens with God distancing God's self from the people until they decide to make reparation (5:15). This strategy is different from the previous one that promises divine wrath (5:8-14).

Speakers shift from God to Hosea in 6:1-3, a song of penitence, where Hosea exhorts the people to return to God, who will act with compassion to restore and renew them (6:1-2). Hosea also encourages the Israelites to renew their relationship with their God (6:3).

Speakers shift again in Hosea 6:4–7:2. In 6:4-6, the poet features God addressing both Israel and Judah. God directs two rhetorical questions to the two kingdoms to express divine frustration and bewilderment (6:4a). Then, with metaphorical language taken from the natural world, God declares to them the instability and unreliability of their love (6:4b), which, according to covenant, should be loyal and steadfast. Seeing their condition, God next recounts what has been done in the past on their behalf, namely, the exercise of punitive divine justice. The people's disloyalty (6:4) is what has provoked divine wrath (6:5). The passage reaches its climax in verse 6, a verse that makes a sharp theological statement: Israel's God wants loyalty and knowledge of God instead of sacrifices and burnt offerings. Ethical living is more important than religious rituals. True worship is not defined solely by ritual practice; rather, it consists of an attitude and way of life characterized by justice, righteousness, and steadfast love—the hallmarks of covenant and the necessary ingredients for right relationships with all creation (cf. Jer 9:24).

In Hosea 6:7-11, God exposes Israel's crimes, which include violating covenant, betrayal (6:7), murder (6:8-9), and idolatry (6:10). The high point of this unit occurs in verse 11, where God also puts Judah on notice. What Judah has sown, that is, evil, Judah will now reap, that is, evil in return that will take the form of divine judgment (cf. Mic 2:1-5). In Hosea 7:1-2 God continues to upbraid Israel, making known to the people that all their wickedness has not gone unseen by God. The healing reference in verse 1 contrasts with Hosea 5:13, where Israel sought healing from Assyria but to no avail. Thus, none of Israel's or Judah's wrongdoings go unseen by their God, and Israel seems to have lost its conscience: "Yet they do not call to mind / that I remember all their wickedness" (7:2a).

DESCRIPTION OF FAILED LEADERSHIP

Hosea 7:3-7

The central simile in Hosea 7:3-7 is a blazing oven that the poet uses to depict the heated rage of those who not only betray their rulers (7:3-5) but also eventually destroy them (7:6-7). The oven to which the prophet refers

Israel's Domestic Politics

³With their wickedness they make
　　the king rejoice,
　　the princes too, with their
　　　　treacherous deeds.
⁴They are all adulterers,
　　like a blazing oven,
Which the baker quits stoking,
　　after the dough's kneading until
　　　　its rising.
⁵On the day of our king,
　　they made the princes sick with
　　　　poisoned wine;
　　he extended his hand to the
　　　　scoffers.
⁶For they draw near in ambush
　　with their hearts like an oven.
All the night their anger sleeps;
　　in the morning it flares like a
　　　　blazing fire.

⁷They are all heated like ovens,
　　and consume their rulers.
All their kings have fallen;
　　none of them calls upon me.

Israel's Foreign Politics

⁸Ephraim is mixed with the nations,
　　Ephraim is an unturned cake.
⁹Strangers have consumed his
　　　　strength,
　　but he does not know it;
Gray hairs are strewn on his head,
　　but he takes no notice of it.
¹⁰The arrogance of Israel bears
　　witness against him;
　　yet they do not return to the
　　　　LORD, their God,
　　nor seek him, despite all this.
¹¹Ephraim is like a dove,
　　silly and senseless;

---

was round with a stone or earthen floor. Its dome was made of hardened clay. To whom the king (7:5) and kings (7:7) refer is unclear. Possibilities among those assassinated in Hosea's day include Zechariah (746 B.C.), Shallum (746 B.C.), Pekahiah (737 B.C.), and Pekah (732 B.C.). The oven simile comes into full view in verse 7. Just like one who eats bread from a heated oven, so the conspirators "consume their rulers" (7:7a), which causes the kings to fall (7:7b). The most crucial statement of the passage occurs at the end of verse 7, where God states, "none of them calls upon me." In the midst of Israel's political, social, and religious chaos, the people fail to call upon their God and to rely on God, who is Lord of creation and Lord of history. This God would have come to their aid. Instead, they turn to others. Even the kings themselves believed in their own power as the ultimate source of power and wisdom and failed to recognize God's sovereignty. In sum, Israel has serious internal problems.

DESCRIPTION OF ISRAEL'S FOLLY AND FATE

Hosea 7:8-12

The focus now shifts from Israel's domestic problems that involve conspiracy and assassination (7:3-7) to Israel's alliances with foreign power

They call upon Egypt,
 they go to Assyria.
¹²When they go I will spread my net
 around them,
 like birds in the air I will bring
 them down.*
I will chastise them when I hear
 of their assembly.
¹³Woe to them, for they have
 strayed from me!
Ruin to them, for they have
 rebelled against me!
Though I wished to redeem them,
 they spoke lies against me.
¹⁴They have not cried to me from
 their hearts
when they wailed upon their
 beds;
For wheat and wine they lacerated
 themselves;
 they rebelled against me.
¹⁵Though I trained and strengthened
 their arms,
 yet they devised evil against me.
¹⁶They have again become useless,
 they have been like a treacherous
 bow.
Their princes shall fall by the sword
 because of the insolence of their
 tongues;
thus they shall be mocked in the
 land of Egypt.

and politics. Comparing Israel to an "unturned cake," to a "silly and sense-less" dove, and to "birds in the air" in general captures the kingdom's sordid state (7:8, 11, 12). Pride and arrogance blind Israel (7:10). Because of these two vices, the people refuse to return to God (7:10), who is their true strength, power, and freedom. As a result of its alliances with foreign powers, and with Egypt and Assyria in particular (7:11), Israel loses both strength and independence. The people's folly will reap them an unfortunate fate (7:12).

WOE SPEECH AGAINST ISRAEL

Hosea 7:13-16

This woe speech develops the earlier picture of Israel's fickleness. Instead of trusting in God, Israel trusts in foreign alliances that, in the end, cannot help Israel in its time of dire need. Israel, because of its poor choices, now stands condemned by God, who is angered by the people's disloyalty, rebellion, betrayal, and evil deeds (7:13-15). The anger of God is both personal and poignant: "they have strayed from me"; "they have rebelled against me"; "they spoke lies against me" (7:13); "They have not cried to me from their hearts"; they rebelled against me" (7:14); "they devised evil against me" (7:15). A people full of potential have now become "useless" and like a "treacherous bow" (7:16a). Israel's rulers are destined for destruction and mockery (7:16b) by the very nation in whom they had trusted.

Corruption of Cult, Domestic and Foreign Politics

8 ¹Put the trumpet to your lips!
    One like an eagle is over the
        house of the LORD!
Because they have violated my
        covenant,
    and rebelled against my law,
²They cry out to me,
    "My God! We know you!"
³But Israel has rejected what is
        good;
    the enemy shall pursue him.

⁴They made kings, but not by my
        authority;

they established princes, but
    without my knowledge.
With their silver and gold
    they made idols for themselves,
    to their own destruction.
⁵He has rejected your calf, Samaria!
    My wrath is kindled against
        them;
How long will they be incapable of
        innocence in Israel?
⁶An artisan made it,
    it is no god at all.
The calf of Samaria
    will be dashed to pieces.

⁷When they sow the wind,
    they will reap the whirlwind;

DECLARATION OF WARFARE

Hosea 8:1-14

Hosea 8:1-14 continues the theme of Israel's idolatry. Comprised of three units—verses 1-3, a cry of warning; verses 4-13, a description of Israel's political and cultic transgressions; and verse 14, a statement of divine judgment—this passage is a vivid example of Israel's breach of covenant relationship and blatant disregard for torah. Similar to Isaiah 1:2-9, Jeremiah 4:1-17, and Ezekiel 6:1-7, it elicits further ethical and theological reflection with respect to the statement of divine judgment in verse 14.

Verses 1-3, the first unit, set the stage for the sequence of events that follow, all of which lead up to the statement of divine judgment in verse 14. Verse 1a opens with a strong imperative spoken by God through the prophet and addressed to an individual: "Put the trumpet to your lips!" The remainder of the verse states the reason for the alarm, "One like an eagle is over the house of the LORD" (8:1ab), and why the people are in danger: "Because they have violated my covenant, / and rebelled against my law" (8:1b). Here, "law" refers to torah as "instruction," as will be seen in verses 4-13. Members of the Israelite community have not followed the teachings and ways of God. In verse 2, God quotes the community. The statement is ironic since in verse 3 God accuses Israel of spurning the good and because of this, the enemy—the "eagle" (8:1)—will pursue Israel and ironically, this enemy—this vulture—is already over the house of Israel.

Verses 4-13 outline the issues and transgressions that violate covenant and law that lead the Israelites away from torah and away from God. First,

The stalk of grain that forms no
head
can yield no flour;
Even if it could,
strangers would swallow it.
⁸Israel is swallowed up;
now they are among the nations,
like a useless vessel.
⁹For they went up to Assyria—
a wild ass off on its own—
Ephraim bargained for lovers.
¹⁰Even though they bargain with
the nations,
I will now gather them together;

They will soon succumb
under the burden of king and
princes.

¹¹When Ephraim made many altars
to expiate sin,
they became altars for sinning.
¹²Though I write for him my many
instructions,
they are considered like a
stranger's.
¹³They love sacrifice,
they sacrifice meat and eat it,
but the LORD is not pleased with
them.

Israel set up kings independent of God, and princes without God's knowledge. The community had been instructed by God through Moses that the people could indeed set up a king but the person had to be one chosen by God (Deut 17:14-15; see also 1 Sam 16:1-13; 2 Sam 5:3; 1 Kgs 1:11, 18; 19:15-16). Furthermore, the community not only chose a king by themselves but also set up princes without God's knowledge. Hence, political leadership was established without divine initiation, consultation, or approval. Such acts violate covenant.

The indictment against Israel for its idolatry comes in verse 4b: "With their silver and gold / they made idols for themselves." Idolatry violates the law (see Exod 20:3-4; 34:17; Lev 19:4) and goes against the sense of covenant of which the law is a part. Both covenant and law forbade the construction and worship of idols (see Deut 4:23 and Hos 8:1b).

Verses 5-6 with their reference to the calf of Samaria recall Exodus 32:1-35, when the Israelites made a golden calf from their jewelry while Moses was on Mount Sinai. The verses are addressed to the people of Samaria, the capital city of the northern kingdom, Israel. The "calf of Samaria" (8:6) is to be understood as the bull that Jeroboam I had erected in Bethel (1 Kgs 12:29). The bull is the symbol for the Canaanite god Baal. Just as the people have spurned the good, namely, God and God's ways, so God will reject the people's calf and break it to pieces. Thus, the Israelites live under the shadow of God's judgment, a theme that continues in the next three verses of the passage.

Verses 7-10 describe Israel's political situation. The country is powerless (8:8). Israel has offered tribute to Assyria before the Assyrian invasion, and conquest made it obligatory (8:8-9). Furthermore, Ephraim—the northern

Now he will remember their guilt	Judah, too, has fortified many
and punish their sins;	cities,
they shall return to Egypt.	but I will send fire upon his
¹⁴Israel has forgotten his maker	cities,
and has built palaces.	to devour their strongholds.

kingdom Israel—has "bargained for lovers" (8:9). Despite Israel's negotiations with other countries, it will have to endure God's judgment: God will gather the people up, and they will suffer under the burden of corrupt kings and princes not of their own country (8:10). The verses foreshadow Israel's deportation to Assyria, which, for the Israelite people, could be interpreted as God's curse and judgment for the breach of covenant and the violation of torah (see Deut 28:36-37).

Verses 11-13 shed light on Israel's religious practices and cultic sins. Verse 12, a pivotal verse, features the unit's main point: Israel has disregarded torah—God's instructions are looked upon as a strange thing. Thus, the multiple altars for the expiation of sins become altars of sinning (8:11), and the sacrifices offered to God are consequently rejected by God (8:13a). In verse 13b, divine judgment is cast upon Israel: God will remember the people's iniquity, punish their sins, and they will return to Egypt, to the place where they had once experienced bondage.

The passage closes on a somber note (8:14). Amnesia is the root of all Israel's problems. Israel has forgotten its God and has taken refuge in political and military strength by means of building palaces and multiplying fortified cities. The false security will, however, end in folly at the moment of divine judgment when fire will consume the strongholds.

In summary, Hosea 8:1-14 provides a vivid picture of Israel and its struggles. The nation is (1) guilty of idolatry, (2) considered useless by other nations, (3) disloyal, (4) hypocritical, (5) forgetful, and (6) living under divine judgment. Israel has broken covenant and transgressed the law. For readers then and now, the prophet delivers a powerful message, and yet, one is given to question the ethical aspect of the prophet's word that promises destruction in the face of infidelity.

JUDGMENT SPEECH AGAINST ISRAEL

Hosea 9:1-6

The poet opens this next passage on a somber note. God, the speaker, tells the people not to rejoice or exult like the nations (9:1). Because Israel has abandoned God, Israel will be made to suffer in a myriad of ways: there

From Days of Celebration to Days of Punishment

9 ¹Do not rejoice, Israel,
    do not exult like the nations!
For you have prostituted yourself,
    abandoning your God,
    loving a prostitute's fee
    upon every threshing floor.
²Threshing floor and wine press
    will not nourish them,
    the new wine will fail them.

³They will not dwell in the LORD's
    land;
    Ephraim will return to Egypt,
    and in Assyria they will eat
        unclean food.
⁴They will not pour libations of
    wine to the LORD,
    and their sacrifices will not
        please him.
Their bread will be like mourners'
    bread,
that makes unclean all who eat
    of it;
Their food will be for their own
    appetites;
    it cannot enter the house of the
        LORD.

⁵What will you do on the festival
    day,
    the day of the LORD's feast?
⁶When they flee from the
    devastation,
    Egypt will gather them,
        Memphis will bury them.
Weeds will overgrow their silver
    treasures,
    and thorns, their tents.

⁷They have come, the days of
    punishment!
    they have come, the days of
        recompense!
Let Israel know it!
    "The prophet is a fool,
    the man of the spirit is mad!"

will be a lack of nourishment (9:2); they will be deported to Egypt and Assyria, where life will be difficult (9:3); celebration will come to an end; ritual sacrifices will be without merit (9:4), which would render food unclean (cf. Num 19:15; Deut 26:14), like bread eaten by mourners (9:4b; cf. Ezek 4:9-17; 24:17, 22) that is not suitable to enter the house of God (9:4c). The question raised in verse 5 is rhetorical. The festival day could refer to one of three pilgrimage festivals: Passover, Shavuot, or Sukkoth. Sukkoth is the most likely reference (see 1 Kgs 8:2, 65; 12:32-33; Ezra 3:4; 6:22). Finally, when Israel flees to a foreign land for protection, Israel will meet its fate (9:6).

STATEMENT OF IMPENDING DIVINE CHASTISEMENT

Hosea 9:7-9

Having exposed Israel's transgressions, and having passed judgment on the guilty parties, God now announces imminent chastisement upon Israel (9:7a, 9b) because of Israel's great iniquity and hostility (9:7c). The "days of punishment," the "days of recompense," have come (9:7). Furthermore, Israel's prophets are unable to deal with the disaster that the people

Because your iniquity is great,
   great, too, is your hostility.
[8]The watchman of Ephraim, the
   people of my God, is the
   prophet;
   yet a fowler's snare is on all his
      ways,
   hostility in the house of his God.
[9]They have sunk to the depths of
   corruption,
   as in the days of Gibeah;
God will remember their iniquity
   and punish their sins.

From Former Glory to a History of Corruption

[10]Like grapes in the desert,
   I found Israel;
Like the first fruits of the fig tree, its
   first to ripen,

I looked on your ancestors.
But when they came to Baal-peor
   and consecrated themselves to
      the Shameful One,
   they became as abhorrent as the
      thing they loved.
[11]Ephraim is like a bird:
   their glory flies away—
   no birth, no pregnancy, no
      conception.
[12]Even though they bring up their
   children,
   I will make them childless, until
      no one is left.
Indeed, woe to them
   when I turn away from them!
[13]Ephraim, as I saw, was a tree
   planted in a meadow;
But now Ephraim will bring out
   his children to the slaughterer!

---

are about to experience (9:7). The comment in verse 7 is also a word of mockery: Israel's prophets are mocked for their attacks on Hosea. In verse 8 the watchman of Ephraim is Hosea himself, the true prophet, against whom a fowler's snare has been set. The image of the "watchman" in verse 8 is a common one applied to other prophets (cf. Jer 6:17; Ezek 3:17; Isa 56:10). God makes clear that Israel has sunk into "the depths of corruption / as in the days of Gibeah" (9:9). The simile probably refers to the violent and shameful deeds that are recounted in Judges 19–21, where the tribe of Benjamin violated a Levite and his concubine at Gibeah. Because of this crime, Benjamin was almost exterminated.

DESCRIPTION OF ISRAEL'S CRIMES

Hosea 9:10-17

The next unit features a series of contrasts that highlight God's graciousness to Israel's wayward response, which results in stirring up God's frustration and anger that causes painful chastisement. In verses 10-13, 15-16 God is the speaker; in verses 14, 17 Hosea speaks.

9:10-14 Crimes at Baal-peor

The opening similes in verse 10 are common ways of correlating nature with Israel to expose God's care for the Israelites just as farmers care for the

¹⁴Give them, LORD!
  give them what?
Give them a miscarrying womb,
  and dry breasts!
¹⁵All their misfortune began in Gilgal;
  yes, there I rejected them.
Because of their wicked deeds
  I will drive them out of my house.
I will love them no longer;
  all their princes are rebels.
¹⁶Ephraim is stricken,
  their root is dried up;
  they will bear no fruit.

Were they to bear children,
  I would slay the beloved of their
  womb.
¹⁷My God will disown them
  because they have not listened
  to him;
  they will be wanderers among
  the nations.

Destruction of Idolatrous Cultic Objects

10 ¹Israel is a luxuriant vine
  whose fruit matches its growth.

---

first harvest of fruit (cf. Exod 23:19; 34:26; Deut 26:2, 10). The similes communicate a sense of divine nostalgia. Israel was God's "first fruits," and now, just like their ancestors, the Israelites of Hosea's day have turned away from God and are guilty of idolatry just like their ancestors (9:10c). The story associated with Baal-peor can be found in Numbers 25:1-9. At Baal-peor, Israel became involved with the worship of a Moabite fertility god known as Baal of peor. Verse 11 describes Israel's fickleness and points out that their idolatry will not bear fruit (9:12). In verse 13 the poet presents an image of promise and pleasure but immediately a contrast is set up to reiterate the passage's basic themes. Speakers shift in verse 14 from God to Hosea. Hosea's appeal to God in verse 14 exposes the prophet's frustration with the people and reverses the expectations of the fertility feast of Sukkoth and the so-called marital relationship between God and Israel. For Hosea, a miscarrying womb and dry breasts are better than having to watch one's children perish.

9:15-17 Crimes at Gilgal

God once again condemns Israel in verses 15-16. For a rich history associated with Gilgal, see 1 Samuel 11; 13:7-15; Joshua 4:19–5:15; 9–10. At Gigal, a shrine had been erected where Israel practiced idolatrous worship (Hos 4:15; 12:11). The unit closes with Hosea announcing God's utter disgust with Israel (9:17). The announcement foreshadows both deportation and later exile.

THREE METAPHORS CONCERNING ISRAEL

Hosea 10:1–11:11

Hosea 10:1–11:11 is composed of three units resplendent in metaphorical language that continues earlier themes heard in the book of Hosea, specifically,

The more abundant his fruit,
the more altars he built;
The more productive his land,
the more sacred pillars he set up.
²Their heart is false!
Now they will pay for their
guilt:
God will break down their altars
and destroy their sacred pillars.
³For now they will say,
"We have no king!
Since we do not fear the Lord,
the king—what could he do for
us?"
⁴They make promises,
swear false oaths, and make
covenants,
While lawsuits sprout
like poisonous weeds in the
furrows of a field!
⁵The inhabitants of Samaria are
afraid

for the calf of Beth-aven;
Its people mourn for it
and its idolatrous priests wail
over it,
—over its glory which has
departed from it.
⁶It too will be carried to Assyria,
as an offering to the great king.
Ephraim will be put to shame,
Israel will be shamed by his
schemes.

⁷Samaria and her king will
disappear,
like a twig upon the waters.
⁸The high places of Aven will be
destroyed,
the sin of Israel;
thorns and thistles will overgrow
their altars.
Then they will cry out to the
mountains, "Cover us!"
and to the hills, "Fall upon us!"

God's care for Israel and Israel's idolatrous, apostate, and rebellious nature. The most poignant of all three units (10:1-10; 10:11-15; 11:1-11) is Hosea 11:1-11, a window into the divine heart.

10:1-10 Israel as a luxuriant vine

In Hosea 10:1-10 the poet features God as the speaker, who once again uses natural world imagery to describe Israel's beauty and depravity (cf. Hos 9:10; Isa 5:1-7). The opening verse (10:1) recalls Israel's past when Israel lived in the midst of economic prosperity. The fruit-yielding vine may be a reference to the days of Jeroboam II (786–746 B.C.). The main point in the passage is that Israel's "heart is false" (10:2), and because of Israel's duplicitous heart, the altars and the pillars (10:2), the king (10:3), and even the calf will perish (10:5). Here the calf refers to the calf at Bethel that is mockingly called the "calf of Beth-aven" (10:5), which will be carried to Assyria as tribute to the Assyrian king (10:6a). As a whole, the unit foreshadows the Assyrian invasion and consequential deportation of many of the Israelites to Assyria (10:6-7). The kingdom of Israel will soon stand exposed before God and the nations, and especially before Assyria, without any security or cover available to them (10:8).

War Because of Israel's Wickedness

⁹Since the days of Gibeah
 you have sinned, Israel.
There they took their stand;
 will war not reach them in
 Gibeah?
Against a perverse people
 ¹⁰I came and I chastised them;
Peoples will be gathered against
 them
 when I bind them to their two
 crimes.
¹¹Ephraim was a trained heifer,
 that loved to thresh;
I myself laid a yoke
 upon her beautiful neck;
I will make Ephraim break ground,
 Judah must plow,
 Jacob must harrow for himself:
¹²"Sow for yourselves justice,
 reap the reward of loyalty;
Break up for yourselves a new field,
 for it is time to seek the LORD,
 till he comes and rains justice
 upon you."
¹³But you have plowed wickedness,
 reaped perversity,

and eaten the fruit of falsehood.
Because you have trusted in your
 own power,
 and in your many warriors,
¹⁴The clamor of war shall break out
 among your people
and all your fortresses shall be
 ravaged
As Salman ravaged Beth-arbel on
 the day of war,
 smashing mothers along with
 their children.
¹⁵So it will be done to you, Bethel,
 because of your utter
 wickedness:
At dawn the king of Israel
 will utterly disappear.

The Disappointment of a Parent

11 ¹When Israel was a child I loved
 him,
 out of Egypt I called my son.
²The more I called them,
 the farther they went from me,
Sacrificing to the Baals
 and burning incense to idols.

10:11-15 Israel as a trained heifer

In these verses the poet uses agricultural life to beckon Israel to return to God, but God's plea goes unheard and unheeded. In verse 12 the poet characterizes God as one calling out to the people of Israel, imploring them to seek the Lord, but nothing moves these wayward ones among the Israelites to change their ways. Thus, the consequences of war will befall them; the Assyrians will invade the land. Here, the Assyrian invasion foreshadowed in verses 14-15 is historically and politically inevitable but portrayed in the text as a form of divine punishment. The poet shows us that even the threat of war does not provoke Israel to change its course of life.

11:1-11 Israel as a child

Hosea 11:1-11 is a poem that might be described as the window to God's heart. Here the poet discloses what could be termed the vacillation of God's heart. In verses 1-4 God remembers how, when Israel was a child, God loved Israel, but how Israel moved farther and farther away, choosing to

³Yet it was I who taught Ephraim to
walk,
who took them in my arms;
but they did not know that I
cared for them.
⁴I drew them with human cords,
with bands of love;
I fostered them like those
who raise an infant to their
cheeks;
I bent down to feed them.
⁵He shall return to the land of
Egypt,
Assyria shall be his king,
because they have refused to
repent.
⁶The sword shall rage in his cities:
it shall destroy his diviners,
and devour them because of
their schemings.
⁷My people have their mind set on
apostasy;

though they call on God in
unison,
he shall not raise them up.

But Love Is Stronger and Restores

⁸How could I give you up,
Ephraim,
or deliver you up, Israel?
How could I treat you as Admah,
or make you like Zeboiim?
My heart is overwhelmed,
my pity is stirred.
⁹I will not give vent to my blazing
anger,
I will not destroy Ephraim
again;
For I am God and not a man,
the Holy One present among
you;
I will not come in wrath.
¹⁰They shall follow the Lord,
who roars like a lion;

sacrifice to the Baals and offer incense to idols (11:1-2). The poet uses the metaphor of a parent and child to compare God's relationship with Israel. The allusion to being called out of Egypt (11:1) harks back to the exodus story, where the intimate relationship between God and the Israelites first began. In verses 3-4 the poet next describes God's nurturing and parental love for Israel and provides a contrast to Israel's rejection of God's tender love (11:2). Thus, verses 1-4 provide a glimpse into the heartwarming, heartrending relationship that God has with Israel. God is the one who is "long-suffering" in the relationship, the one who faithfully cares for Israel despite Israel's lack of appreciation of the gift.

In verses 5-7 the poem's focus and tone shift. With love unreturned, God now vows to send Israel back to its days of oppression, which, paradoxically, may already have been occurring (11:6). Verse 7 describes God's frustration with Israel. Verse 8 expresses the folly associated with calling on false gods. Thus far, the poet has portrayed God in a very personable and human way, as one who loves Israel deeply but who gets aggravated with the people's lack of responsiveness and apostasy.

In verses 8-9 the tone shifts again. God uses a series of rhetorical questions to engage in self-reflection. God wonders how Israel could ever be

When he roars,
 his children shall come
  frightened from the west,
¹¹Out of Egypt they shall come
  trembling, like birds,
 like doves, from the land of
  Assyria;
And I will resettle them in their
  homes,
 oracle of the LORD.

Infidelity of Israel

12 ¹Ephraim has surrounded me
   with lies,
 the house of Israel, with deceit;
Judah still wanders about with
  gods,
 and is faithful to holy ones.
²Ephraim shepherds the wind,
 and pursues the east wind all
  day long.

He multiplies lies and violence:
 They make a covenant with
  Assyria,
 and oil is carried to Egypt.

³The LORD has a dispute with
  Judah,
 and will punish Jacob for his
  conduct,
 and repay him for his deeds.
⁴In the womb he supplanted his
  brother,
 and in his vigor he contended
  with a divine being;
⁵He contended with an angel and
  prevailed,
 he wept and entreated him.
At Bethel he met with him,
 and there he spoke with him.
⁶The LORD is the God of hosts,
 the LORD is his name!

given up, how Israel could ever be handed over, how God could ever make or treat Israel like others. Verse 8c provides a glimpse of God's deepest feelings: God's heart recoils; God's compassion grows tender and warm. Because of God's recoiling heart and warm and tender compassion, God will not execute fierce anger or take any other measures of chastisement (11:9a). The verse ends with a divine self-confession: Israel's God is no mortal; Israel's God is the Holy One in the midst of the Israelites; Israel's God "will not come in wrath" (11:9b).

The poem presents a very human portrait of a loving God with intense feelings for Israel. Throughout many of the passages studied thus far, God has been depicted as possessing many human and culturally conditioned qualities. Sometimes these have prompted the question, "To what extent is God accurately portrayed in and by the biblical text, or to what extent is the texts' depiction merely a projected, historically and culturally limited, image of God?" Verse 9 presents God not coming in wrath or violence but rather, in spite of Israel's unfaithfulness (11:7), God will come with love and compassion. God will refrain from violence. A challenge to traditional Deuteronomistic theology of retribution, verse 9 makes clear that the unfaithful will not receive the punishment their unfaithfulness has warranted; rather, God, despite their offense, will not execute power against them. Is this not an attractive portrait of God, one that, while depicting God's love

⁷You must return to your God.
Maintain loyalty and justice
and always hope in your God.

⁸A merchant who holds a false
balance,
he loves to extort!
⁹Ephraim has said,
"How rich I have become;
I have made a fortune!"
All his gain will not suffice
for the guilt of his sin.
¹⁰I the LORD have been your God,
since the land of Egypt;
I will again have you live in tents,
as on feast days.
¹¹I spoke to the prophets,
I granted many visions,
and through the prophets I told
parables.
¹²In Gilead is falsehood, they have
come to nothing;
in Gilgal they sacrifice bulls,
But their altars are like heaps of
stones
in the furrows of the field.
¹³Jacob fled to the land of Aram,
and Israel served for a wife;
for a wife he tended sheep.

in human terms, depicts God as not human in refraining from anger and destruction? Thus, in this text the poet provides a vision to which humans, then and now, might well aspire.

In the conclusion of the poem, the poet depicts God metaphorically. God is a lion who roars, whose "children" come frightened from the west like birds from Egypt and like doves from Assyria (11:10-11). God will resettle the Israelites in their homes (11:11). With Israel's return from Egypt and Assyria, the exile (11:5) is reversed. Although verses 10-11 convey hope, they depict God as a ferocious father and the Israelites as children who shake at their father's beckoning. This father-child imagery recalls similar imagery that appeared earlier in the poem, but for modern readers, it suggests a patriarchal and paternalistic relationship, one that betrays religious and cultural attitudes present in Israelite society during the eighth century B.C. and later.

In summary, in Hosea 11:1-11 the poet conveys a very human and divine image of God, but one that is not without its flaws. Central to the passage is the language of relationship—the language of a vacillating heart that moves back and forth from care to frustration to care and compassion with the promise of future restoration. The passage depicts a loving God whose love transcends human love and who will not harm the beloved.

DESCRIPTION OF ISRAEL'S INFIDELITY

Hosea 12:1–13:1

This unit captures many of the themes expressed thus far in the book of Hosea. In the face of God's faithful, gracious love, some among the people

¹⁴But by a prophet the LORD
  brought Israel out of Egypt,
  and by a prophet Israel was
    tended.
¹⁵Ephraim has aroused bitter anger,
  so his Lord shall cast his blood-
    guilt upon him
  and repay him for his scorn.

The Death of Ephraim

13 ¹When Ephraim spoke there was
    terror;
  he was exalted in Israel;
  but he became guilty through
    Baal and died.

²Now they continue to sin,
  making for themselves molten
    images,
Silver idols according to their skill,
  all of them the work of artisans.
"To these, offer sacrifice," they say.
  People kiss calves!
³Therefore, they will be like a
    morning cloud
  or like the dew that vanishes
    with the dawn,
Like chaff storm-driven from the
    threshing floor
  or like smoke out of the window.

---

of both Israel and Judah have forsaken God and have acted foolishly (12:1-2). Hosea 12:3-7 takes the form of a lawsuit whereby God lays out the case against the two kingdoms (12:3-6) and ends with a strong word of divine exhortation (12:7). Embedded in the lawsuit is a recitation of the Jacob tradition with specific allusions to Genesis 25:19-26; 27:36; 32:27-29. Hosea 12:8-11 continues to describe the foolhardiness of Israel despite God's intervention with prophets (12:11, 14), whom God used to assist, instruct, and woo back the people. God's anger now seems justified but how that anger will be expressed reflects both an underlying theological agenda that reflects the Deuteronomic theology of retribution (see Deut 28) and, perhaps, the poet's desire to pose an incredible divine threat in order to scare the guilty parties into change and reform (12:15). Either way, the historical outcome of the times shows us that such tactics are ineffectual in dealing with a people whose hearts have been hardened and who are caught up in ways that do not lead to and foster right relationship. The passage concludes with a turn of events for Israel that foreshadows the collapse and destruction of the northern kingdom (13:1).

JUDGMENT SPEECH AGAINST ISRAEL

Hosea 13:2–14:1

The poet has announced God's judgment upon Israel, who now lives under divine threat (13:1), and yet, those guilty of transgression continue on in their wayward deeds of idolatry (13:2). Once again, the poet features God threatening to deliver punitive chastisement, a message cast in four descriptive similes (13:3). The voice of Israel's God as the sovereign one,

⁴I, the Lord, am your God,
  since the land of Egypt;
Gods apart from me you do not
    know;
  there is no savior but me.
⁵I fed you in the wilderness,
  in the parched land.
⁶When I fed them, they were
    satisfied;
  when satisfied, they became
    proud,
  therefore they forgot me.
⁷So, I will be like a lion to them,
  like a leopard by the road I will
    keep watch.
⁸I will attack them like a bear
    robbed of its young,
  and tear their hearts from their
    breasts;
I will devour them on the spot like
  a lion,
  as a wild animal would rip them
    open.

⁹I destroy you, Israel!
  who is there to help you?
¹⁰Where now is your king,
  that he may rescue you?
And all your princes,
  that they may defend you?

Of whom you said,
  "Give me a king and princes"?
¹¹I give you a king in my anger,
  and I take him away in my
    wrath.

¹²The guilt of Ephraim is wrapped
    up,
  his sin is stored away.
¹³The birth pangs will come for him,
  but this is an unwise child,
Who, when it is time, does not
    present himself
  at the mouth of the womb.
¹⁴Shall I deliver them from the
    power of Sheol?
  shall I redeem them from death?
Where are your plagues, O death!
  where is your sting, Sheol!
  Compassion is hidden from my
    eyes.

¹⁵Though Ephraim may flourish
    among his brothers,
  an east wind will come, a wind
    from the Lord,
  rising from the wilderness,
That will dry up his spring,
  and leave his fountain dry.
It will loot his treasury
  of every precious thing.

---

scorned by the people despite the many acts of divine graciousness and tender care (13:4-6), bellows loudly. The one who shepherded Israel will now become a lion, a leopard, poised to attack the people with the ferociousness of a mother bear who has been robbed of her cubs (13:6-8a). The attack will be ruthless and lethal (13:8). The poet's images are horrific, and although they are used to stage divine rage, we need to remember that such texts are imaginatively poetic with a message and purpose directed toward the original audience of the proclamations, living in extremely violent times. The images are images of conquest that reflect the reality of the brutal Assyrian invasion into the northern kingdom Israel in 722 b.c. These images commonly appear in descriptions of brutal oppressors (cf. 2 Kgs 8:12; Isa 13:16, 18; Nah 3:10).

14 ¹Samaria has become guilty,
for she has rebelled against her
God.
They shall fall by the sword,
their infants shall be dashed to
pieces,
their pregnant women shall be
ripped open.

Sincere Conversion and New Life

²Return, Israel, to the LORD, your
God;
you have stumbled because of
your iniquity.
³Take with you words,
and return to the LORD;
Say to him, "Forgive all iniquity,
and take what is good.
Let us offer the fruit of our lips.
⁴Assyria will not save us,
nor will we mount horses;
We will never again say, 'Our god,'
to the work of our hands;

for in you the orphan finds
compassion."
⁵I will heal their apostasy,
I will love them freely;
for my anger is turned away
from them.
⁶I will be like the dew for Israel:
he will blossom like the lily;
He will strike root like the Lebanon
cedar,
⁷and his shoots will go forth.
His splendor will be like the olive
tree
and his fragrance like Lebanon
cedar.
⁸Again they will live in his shade;
they will raise grain,
They will blossom like the vine,
and his renown will be like the
wine of Lebanon.
⁹Ephraim! What more have I to do
with idols?
I have humbled him, but I will
take note of him.

DIVINE PLEA AND PROMISE OF HEALING, RESTORATION, AND NEW LIFE

Hosea 14:2-9

The divine compassion expressed in Hosea 11:1-9 continues in 14:5-9, a divine promise. In verse 5, God promises to heal the Israelites' infidelity and to "love them freely." In verses 6-8, God promises to be "like the dew for Israel"; Israel in turn will "blossom like the lily," "strike root like the Lebanon cedar" (14:6), become beautiful "like the olive tree," smell "like Lebanon cedar" (14:7), "live in [God's] shade," "raise grain," "blossom like the vine," and smell "like the wine of Lebanon" (14:8). Here God resembles Baal, the rain god of fertility. God is about to water Israel to make the land flourish. Verse 9 describes God as an evergreen cypress, from which Israel's faithfulness originates. God, not Baal, is responsible for Israel's future life.

The verses depict God as the sustainer, nurturer, and transformer of life who offers hope to all. Israel is portrayed by means of flourishing natural world imagery. There is a relationship between the restoration of human

I am like a verdant cypress tree.
From me fruit will be found for
you!

Epilogue

[10]Who is wise enough to understand these things?

Who is intelligent enough to
know them?
Straight are the paths of the LORD,
the just walk in them,
but sinners stumble in them.

---

life and the restoration of the natural world. The text portrays a sense of beauty and peace and speaks to the relationship that God and the Israelite people have with creation. For contemporary readers, the text offers a refreshing message that God desires reconciliation and the well-being and fruitfulness of all creation.

EPILOGUE: A WORD OF EXHORTATION

Hosea 14:10

The poet draws the book of Hosea to a close with a simple exhortation to readers. Those who are wise and perceptive will come to understand the ways of God as laid out in the Hosean text, and they will walk in those ways. Those who are transgressors, who continue in the transgression despite the instruction that has been given through the book of Hosea, will stumble in their own paths. The verse reflects the vocabulary of the wisdom tradition and is most likely the hand of a later editor. In sum, the book of Hosea beckons its readers to remain faithful to covenant, faithful to torah, and faithful to God, who, in the end, waits to forgive, to heal, to renew, and to restore (14:2-9).

Micah

Railing against the people of Israel and Judah, Micah of Moresheth, the prophet in the book of Micah, is without guile or fear. He does not cower from addressing the power brokers of his day, and he goes to great lengths to make his message heard, even to the point of being willing to run barefoot and naked through the streets. Singing songs of lamentation and proclaiming words of woe, the prophet foreshadows what is about to befall the Israelite community if people do not change their sordid ways. His message, however, is not all doom and gloom. His vision of the mountain of the Lord's house (4:1-4) where all peoples, all nations, will gather and live in abiding peace with mutual respect is a vision that brings hope not only to the people of Micah's day but also to all who continue to listen and ponder his word today. Micah redefines right relationship and makes clear that offering eternal sacrifices to atone for transgression is not what God desires. Instead, God desires ethical praxis and a change of heart and attitude best expressed through acting justly and loving tenderly, the foundation of which is a humble walk with God, which, transformative in itself, will provide the strength and direction needed for right relationship (6:6-8). Perhaps the greatest of all Micah's proclamations comes at the end of the book, where the prophet proclaims who Israel's God truly is—a God of compassion who casts all sins into the depths of the sea and remains faithful and loving toward all people, all creation, for all times (7:18-20).

The world of Micah

The book of Micah presents itself as a word addressed to the people of Israel and Judah in the latter half of the eighth century B.C. during the reigns of Jotham (742–735 B.C.), Ahaz (735–715 B.C.), and Hezekiah (715–686 B.C.). According to the text of Micah, the prophet's career appears expansive but most likely the prophetic activity was confined to the last quarter of the century during the reign of Hezekiah. Together with Amos, Isaiah, and Hosea, Micah was one of the four great prophets of the eighth century B.C. His name means "who is like the Lord." Micah's name was a common one

during his time but the phrase "of Moresheth" distinguished him from others who bore the same name.

The book itself reflects a period in Israel and Judah's history that was plagued by Assyrian military invasions. These invasions began with the Syro-Ephraimite War (734–732 B.C.) and continued down through Sennacherib's invasion of Judah in 701 B.C. In the midst of such unrest, Judah did experience religious reforms and an economic revolution. These changes allowed the wealthy landowners to grow in prosperity at the expense of small peasant farmers. Soon religious and political leaders began to view their vocations and positions as business careers. Instead of focusing on serving the people in the communities, they began to assert their power for self-serving purposes and had little regard for the common good. With the abuse of power and idolatry on the rise, right relationship with God and with one another was compromised and gave way to injustice, oppression, and corruption. Assyria was at its zenith of power and influence as Babylon increased in strength. The northern kingdom Israel and the southern kingdom Judah were ripe for invasion. The prophet Micah read the signs of the times, only to have the inevitable eventually occur—the collapse and destruction of the two kingdoms. This catastrophe resulted in Israel's inhabitants being deported to Assyria and, later, Judah's inhabitants being exiled to Babylon and Egypt. Into this climate of unrest stepped the prophet Micah, one "filled with power, / with the spirit of the LORD, / with justice and with might; / To declare to Jacob his crimes / and to Israel his sins" (3:8). Ultimately, Micah held out hope to a people loved dearly by their God.

The literary dimensions of the book of Micah

The literary composition of the book of Micah has intrigued scholars for years. In general, scholars have used either a diachronic or synchronic approach to the study of the text, along with other methods of criticism, all of which have yielded many fruitful insights and readings of the text. Much of the contemporary research has focused on the literary and rhetorical coherence and unity of the book as a whole.

With respect to the structure of the book, several proposals have been offered. Based on the literary content and its theological message, the book can be divided as follows:

I. Superscription (1:1)
II. Proclamation of judgment; word of hope (1:2–3:12)
    Judgment speech (1:2-7)
    Dirge-lament (1:8-16)

The prophet Micah, sculpted by Aleijadinho, in front of the church of the Sanctuary of Bom Jesus of Matosinhos at Congonhas, Minas Gerais, Brazil.

Woe proclamation (2:1-5)
Disputation prophecy (2:6-11)
Salvation proclamation (2:12-13)
Address to Israel's political leadership (3:1-4)
Proclamation concerning the prophets (3:5-7)
Interlude: statement of confidence (3:8)
Address to Israel's leadership (3:9-12)
III. Proclamation of future restoration (4:1–5:14)
Prophetic vision (4:1-5)
Divine promise (4:6–5:14)
IV. Words of judgment, lament, trust (6:1–7:20)
Covenant lawsuit (6:1-5)
Torah liturgy (6:6-8)
Judgment speech (6:9-16)
Lament (7:1-6)
Statement of trust (7:7-10)
Divine promise (7:11-13)
Petition (7:14-17)
Statement of divine love (7:18-20)

As a work of literature, Micah 1–3 is generally accepted as authentic Micah material, though Micah 2:12-13 could be received as a later addition, but evidence remains inconclusive. Micah 6:1–7:6 may also be authentic Micah material, with the remainder of the book consisting of an assortment of later additions. Although some of the contents in the book of Micah have been considered authentic Micah material, the larger question remains: Is the prophet Micah truly a historical person or a literary persona representative of a school of prophets that lived and were active during the mid-eighth century B.C.? Scholars continue to debate the question. The fabric of the book as a whole features a wide array of literary forms and techniques such as judgment speeches (1:2-7; 3:1-2), laments (1:8-16; 7:1-7), a lawsuit (6:1-5), prayers (7:14-17, 18-20), reflections (6:6-8), and metaphors (e.g., 1:2-4; 2:12-13; 3:1-3; 4:1-5, 8-13; 7:1), all of which serve to accent and clarify the prophet's message. Finally, the book of Micah sets out to address Jerusalem and Israel's future in the aftermath of the Babylonian exile.

The theological dimensions of the book of Micah

With creativity and boldness, the prophet Micah addressed not only the social and political issues of his day but also the religious issues, all of which portrayed a picture of gross corruption and injustice. Micah rails against the perpetrators of graft (see, e.g., 1–3) while offering not only a vision of a new world order (see 4:1-5) but also a message of hope (e.g., 2:12-13; 4:6-8). Thus, the book of Micah makes clear that Israel's God will not tolerate injustice and oppression rooted in and flowing from apostasy, idolatry, hypocrisy, the disregard for torah, and the break in covenant relationship. Divine justice will be meted out, and yet, the final word of the book as a whole offers a word of universal compassion (7:18-20), but not before the prophet makes intercession on behalf of the people (6:6-8), which yields one of the most often quoted passages of the entire Bible (6:8).

In addition to a focus on justice, salvation, redemption, and compassion, the book of Micah also presents a multifaceted picture of God. This God can be overpowering (1:2-4), retributive (2:1-3, 4-5), enraged (6:9-16), gracious (2:12-13), instructive (6:8), forgiving, and compassionate (7:18-20), much like human beings. This anthropomorphic and anthropocentric portrayal of God reflects the hand of the human biblical poet and, in many ways, this portrait also reflects the human condition. Israel's God has to be stronger and more powerful than all the people, leaders, and forces of the day. Israel's God has to be sovereign over all other gods as well. Divine sovereignty is a core theological theme in the book of Micah, in the other books of the prophets, and in the Bible as a whole. Perhaps the most prophetic statement that can be made of God is stated in Micah 7:18-20, where the prophet acknowledges the compassion, forgiveness, and fidelity of Israel's God, whose love remains ever constant not just for the people of Micah's day but for all people, all creation, down through the ages, to which life itself bears witness.

Micah

1 ¹The word of the LORD which came to Micah of Moresheth in the days of Jotham, Ahaz, and Hezekiah, kings of Judah, which he saw concerning Samaria and Jerusalem.

I. Oracles of Punishment

²Hear, O peoples, all of you,
  give heed, O earth, and all that
    is in it!

Let the Lord GOD be witness
  against you,
  the Lord from his holy temple!
³For see, the LORD goes out from his
    place
  and descending, treads upon the
    heights of the earth.
⁴The mountains melt under him
  and the valleys split open,
Like wax before the fire,
  like water poured down a slope.

SUPERSCRIPTION

Micah 1:1

The book of Micah opens with a superscription (1:1), typical of many prophetic books (see, e.g., Isa 1:1; Jer 1:1-3; Hos 1:1; Amos 1:1; Zeph 1:1), that situates both prophet and proclamation in a particular time period, and here, specifically in the latter part of the eighth century B.C. All three kings mentioned ruled over Judah. The prophet's proclamation is the result of something that "came" to him, which he "saw" concerning Samaria and Jerusalem, the capital cities of the northern and southern kingdoms, respectfully.

PROCLAMATION OF JUDGMENT; WORD OF HOPE

Micah 1:2–3:12

This first major section of the book includes a proclamation of judgment (1:2–2:11; 3:1-12), and a word of hope (2:12-13).

1:2-7 Judgment speech

In these verses the poet calls his listeners and the whole earth to attention and also calls upon God to be a witness among the inhabitants of the

⁵All this is for the crime of Jacob,
    for the sins of the house of Israel.
What is the crime of Jacob? Is it not
    Samaria?
And what is the sin of the house of
    Judah?
    Is it not Jerusalem?

⁶So I will make Samaria a ruin in
    the field,
    a place to plant vineyards;
I will throw its stones into the valley,
    and lay bare its foundations.
⁷All its carved figures shall be broken
    to pieces,

---

land (1:2). In the Old Testament, God is often called upon to act as a witness (Gen 31:50; 1 Sam 12:5; Jer 42:5). The phrase "from his holy temple" could refer to the temple in Jerusalem/Zion, but here it seems to have in view God's heavenly dwelling place (Ps 11:4) from where God descends.

In metaphorical language, Micah next describes an impending theophany (1:3-4). A theophany is a manifestation of God. The term is derived from two Greek words, "God" and "to show." This theophany highlights the transcendent nature of God. In verse 3 the phrase "the LORD goes out from his place" resumes and advances the thought of verse 2. God who is in the holy temple (1:2) is now going out of that place (1:3). This action on God's part finds an echo in Isaiah 26:21, where God comes out of his place to punish the inhabitants of the earth for their iniquity.

Not only will God go out of the sacred dwelling place but this God will also come down and tread upon the places of the earth. The heights of the earth are sometimes used in connection with God's wrath and sovereignty (Amos 4:1-13). The heights of the earth, literally, "the high places of the earth," is rich in meaning. The Akkadian cognate word for high places means "back, center of the body" (of an animal) but also "ridge" and "high place" as in territory. The high places or "heights of the earth" denoted a certain kind of cultic institution in ancient Israel. These "high places" were homemade constructions most often built on elevated places (Jer 48:35; Isa 15:2) as well as valleys. The houses and shrines of the "high places" were found particularly in the cities of Samaria (1 Kgs 13:32; 2 Kgs 23:19) and in Samaria itself (2 Kgs 17:5-12). The "high places" are associated with apostasy (2 Kgs 23:5-8) and as such are the object of God's wrath (Lev 26:30; 2 Kgs 17:5-23; Ps 78:58).

In Micah 1:3, the meaning of the "heights of the earth" is obscure. The natural assumption would be that they denote the mountains, the "ridges," which are topographically the highest places of the earth. This understanding appears appropriate in light of verse 4. These "high places," however, have a double meaning that becomes clear in verse 5: they will symbolize the capital cities of the northern and southern kingdoms, Samaria

all its wages shall be burned in the fire, and all its idols I will destroy. As the wages of a prostitute it gathered them, and to the wages of a prostitute they shall return.	⁸For this I will lament and wail, go barefoot and naked; I will utter lamentation like the jackals, mourning like the ostriches, ⁹For her wound is incurable; it has come even to Judah.

and Jerusalem, respectfully. Thus, the coming of God is imminent and will have devastating effects, which the poet captures with vivid natural world imagery and a series of similes. These natural world images are metaphors for both kingdoms, which will eventually be destroyed through military invasions. Together, verses 3-4 disclose the power of God and the powerlessness of creation before God.

In verse 4 the focus is on the mountains and the valleys. The "mountains" symbolize permanence, height, and power from primeval times (Ps 90:2; 95:4; Zech 4:7). The "valleys" or "lowlands" are the fruitful, inhabitable areas preferred by people (Judg 1:19, 34; Hos 2:17; Ps 65:14). God's coming, though described in typical theophanic language (see Ps 18:1-19; 97:1-5), will not bring the people what they experienced in the past as God's chosen people (see Judg 5). This time God's coming will bring the unexpected upon them (Mic 1:6-7, 10-16) because of their attitude (Mic 1:5) and deeds (Mic 2:1-11; 3:1-12) and because God is faithful to the divine word.

With two rhetorical questions (1:5), the poet indicts Israel and Judah, and specifically their capital cities, Samaria and Jerusalem. Both cities were associated with idolatry in the latter part of the eighth century B.C. With regard to Samaria, this point becomes clear in Micah 1:6-7. In the capital cities resided the kingdoms' political leadership charged with the responsibility of upholding torah for the sake of the common good. The poet's inference here is that the community is laden with transgressions due to poor leadership (see Mic 3).

In verses 6-7 God, speaking through the prophet, announces a plan to destroy Samaria because of its transgressions, apostasy, and idolatry. By citing Samaria, the poet uses metonymy. Samaria represents Jacob/Israel, the northern kingdom. Samaria's fate symbolizes the fate of the entire kingdom.

Theologically verses 2-7 present a hierarchical and patriarchal picture of an anthropomorphic, anthropocentric God and God's power. This God who dwells in "his holy temple" (1:2) enthroned in the heavenly court will descend and tread "upon the heights of the earth" (1:3), which is quite a

It has reached to the gate of my
   people,
   even to Jerusalem.
¹⁰Do not announce it in Gath,
   do not weep at all;
In Beth-leaphrah
   roll in the dust.
¹¹Pass by,
   you who dwell in Shaphir!
The inhabitants of Zaanan
   do not come forth from their
   city.
There is lamentation in Beth-ezel.
   It will withdraw its support
   from you.
¹²The inhabitants of Maroth
   hope for good,
But evil has come down from the
   LORD
   to the gate of Jerusalem.
¹³Harness steeds to the chariots,
   inhabitants of Lachish;

You are the beginning of sin
   for daughter Zion,
For in you were found
   the crimes of Israel.
¹⁴Therefore you must give back the
   dowry
   to Moresheth-gath;
The houses of Achzib are a dry
   stream bed
   to the kings of Israel.
¹⁵Again I will bring the conqueror
   to you,
   inhabitants of Mareshah;
The glory of Israel shall come
   even to Adullam.
¹⁶Make yourself bald, cut off your
   hair,
   for the children whom you
   cherish;
Make yourself bald as a vulture,
   for they are taken from you into
   exile.

different picture from the God who walked in the garden in the cool of the evening (Gen 3:8) and who spoke with Moses as a friend (Exod 33:11). This God is transcendent and not within reach of the natural world. Such imagery reflects Israel's royal leadership during the monarchical period.

1:8-16 Dirge-lament

Verses 8-16 are a dirge-lament. Verse 8 is a pivotal verse that looks backward to verses 5-7 and forward to verse 9. God "will lament and wail, / go barefoot and naked / . . . utter lamentation like the jackals, / mourning like the ostriches" (1:8) because of the people's transgressions, the impending loss of land and kingdoms, and the sorry state of Jerusalem. "Barefoot and naked" signify mourning (cf. Ezek 24:17-23; Isa 20:2). Nakedness is also associated with sin (see Gen 3:10; 9:20-23). Jackals are smaller than wolves and often prowled among places of ruin and deserted areas. Their food included mammals, poultry, fish, vegetables, carrion, and refuse. They were sensitive to drought and heat and had a distinctive wailing and howl. Ostriches are two-toed, swift, wingless birds that reside in deserted, uninhabited areas (Job 30:29; Isa 13:21; 43:20; Jer 50:39). Both creatures are associated with desolation and, although they can be signs of joy, here they are signs of barrenness. God will perform all of these actions through the

2 ¹Ah! you plotters of iniquity,
    who work out evil on your beds!
In the morning light you carry it out
    for it lies within your power.
²You covet fields, and seize them;
    houses, and take them;
You cheat owners of their houses,
    people of their inheritance.

³Therefore thus says the LORD:
Look, I am planning against this
    family an evil
from which you cannot free
    your necks;
Nor shall you walk with head held
    high,

for it will be an evil time.
⁴On that day you shall be mocked,
    and there will be bitter lament:
"Our ruin is complete,
    our fields are divided among
    our captors,
The fields of my people are
    measured out,
    and no one can get them back!"
⁵Thus you shall have no one
    in the assembly of the LORD
    to allot to you a share of land.

⁶"Do not preach," they preach,
    "no one should preach of these
    things!
Shame will not overtake us."

---

prophet Micah, who is and will be the embodiment of the sinful community. Micah becomes a divine sign for the community and, as prophet, becomes the embodiment of God's presence and God's righteous anger and steadfast love. The incurable wound in verse 9 refers to the blow that Judah and Jerusalem will soon endure, specifically, devastation at the hands of the Babylonians. This incurable wound will be dealt with by God (see Jer 1:14; 15:18; 30:12-15).

Verses 10-15 are the words of the prophet's dirge-lament. They are cast into a funeral song for someone who has already died. All of the cities mentioned are situated in the Shephelah, the lowlands of the region. When God comes down and "treads upon the [high places] of the earth" (1:3), not only will the mountains and hilltops of Samaria and Jerusalem be destroyed but also the lowlands—the Shephelah and all its cities. The historical setting of this dirge-lament is most likely the Assyrian invasion by Sennacherib in 701 B.C. (1:15).

Verse 16 closes the dirge-lament. The verse foreshadows the exile after the fall of Jerusalem in 587 B.C. The use of the perfect tense, otherwise known as the prophetic perfect or tense of vision, for an event that has not yet happened signifies that what has been predicted will, in fact, happen.

2:1-5 Woe proclamation

Chapter 2 opens with a woe proclamation (2:1-5) that conveys a stinging message of judgment. In verse 1 the poet proclaims a warning to those guilty of premeditated injustices, which he enumerates in verse 2.

⁷How can it be said, house of Jacob,
  "Is the LORD short of patience;
  are these the Lord's deeds?"
Do not my words promise good
  to the one who walks in justice?
⁸But you rise up against my people
  as an enemy:
  you have stripped off the gar-
    ment from the peaceful,
From those who go their way in
    confidence,
  as though it were spoils of war.
⁹The women of my people you
    drive out
from their pleasant houses;
From their children you take away
  forever the honor I gave them.

¹⁰"Get up! Leave,
  this is no place to rest";
Because of uncleanness that
    destroys
  with terrible destruction.
¹¹If one possessed of a lying spirit
  speaks deceitfully, saying,
"I will preach to you wine and
    strong drink,"
  that one would be the preacher
    for this people.

Verses 3-5 are an announcement of judgment composed of a proclamation of intended chastisement (2:3), a prediction of disaster (2:4), and a threat (2:5). Here the poet depicts God as a schemer of actions that are going to take place to "get even" with those who have transgressed others. Those who have used power oppressively will experience the chastising of God. Those who have taken land will lose their fields (2:4) and will be banned from any further acquisition of property.

Thus Micah 2:1-5 makes clear that God asserts divine power on behalf of those victimized by the abuse of power by others. Verses 1 and 3 exemplify the principle of *lex talionis* (see Lev 24:18-21), which was part of the Israelites' social and legal culture and which became part of its religious culture.

2:6-11 Disputation prophecy

Verses 6-11 are a disputation prophecy. God speaks through the prophet and quotes the prophet's adversaries. The verses describe the strained relationship that exists between God and some of the Israelites because of their smug attitude (2:6) and their deeds of injustice (2:8-9). The rhetorical question in verse 7 highlights how distant the people have become from their God. Verses 8-9 add new transgressions to the list already begun in 2:1-2. The punishment for treachery is expulsion from the land (2:10). Hence, the people's ill-gotten land will provide no place for the guilty to rest. The land has become "unclean," defiled by the people's wickedness (see Lev 18:24-25). The prophecy closes on a note of sarcasm, which is God's final response to the objection raised by the opponents in verse 6 who do not want to hear an honest prophetic word proclaimed.

12I will gather you, Jacob, each and
every one,
I will assemble all the remnant
of Israel;
I will group them like a flock in the
fold,
like a herd in its pasture;
the noise of the people will
resound.

13The one who makes a breach goes
up before them;
they make a breach and pass
through the gate;
Their king shall go through before
them,
the LORD at their head.

3 1And I said:
Hear, you leaders of Jacob,
rulers of the house of Israel!
Is it not your duty to know what is
right,
2you who hate what is good,
and love evil?
You who tear their skin from them,
and their flesh from their bones;
3Who eat the flesh of my people,
flay their skin from them,
and break their bones;
Who chop them in pieces like flesh
in a kettle,
like meat in a pot.
4When they cry to the LORD,
he will not answer them;

2:12-13 Salvation proclamation

The tone of the poet's message changes in verses 12-13, a salvation proclamation that promises divine care to the exiled ones of the remnant of "Jacob." Here "Jacob" does not refer to the northern kingdom; instead, "Jacob" refers to Judah as the remnant of Israel, which in turn sets the stage for restoration promised in Micah 4–5. The verses will serve as a consolation for when the people are exiled, if only they will remember.

As a whole, Micah 2:1-13 makes several statements. First, the community addressed is struggling and living under divine threat (2:2-11) and divine promise (2:12-13). Second, even those people closest to God are liable to sin and must accept the consequences of their actions. Third, since land is a divine gift, others' property rights and boundaries must be respected (see Exod 20:15, 17 and Deut 15:4-5). Fourth, power, wealth, and status are not to be used to exploit others. Lastly, Israel's God is the sovereign one who will not tolerate apostasy or idolatry; Israel's God is a God of justice who will not tolerate injustice.

3:1-4 Address to Israel's political leadership

Having offered a word of hope, the poet now returns to his proclamation of judgment (3:1-12). This new unit consists of an address to Israel's political leaders (3:1-4). Verses 1-4 can be further subdivided into an accusation (3:1-3) and an announcement of judgment (3:4). In these verses, Micah confronts and condemns Israel's political leaders for their brutal treatment of the kingdom's people. The rhetorical question in verses 1-2 articulates

He will hide his face from them at
  that time,
    because of the evil they have
    done.

⁵Thus says the Lord regarding the
  prophets:
    O you who lead my people
    astray,
When your teeth have something to
  bite
    you announce peace,
But proclaim war against the one
  who fails to put something in
  your mouth.
⁶Therefore you shall have night, not
  vision,
    darkness, not divination;
The sun shall go down upon the
  prophets,

and the day shall be dark for
  them.
⁷Then the seers shall be put to
  shame,
    and the diviners confounded;
They shall all cover their lips,
    because there is no answer from
    God.
⁸But as for me, I am filled with
  power,
    with the spirit of the Lord,
    with justice and with might;
To declare to Jacob his crimes
    and to Israel his sins.

⁹Hear this, you leaders of the house
  of Jacob,
    you rulers of the house of Israel!
You who abhor justice,
    and pervert all that is right;

plainly the sin of Israel's leadership: they do not act justly (3:1); they are haters of good and lovers of evil (3:2). An extended metaphor follows in verses 2b-3, which vivifies the prophet's message and accentuates the leaders' illicit deeds. Here Micah compares Israel's leaders to savage butchers and voracious cannibals who treat people like animals ready to be consumed. The metaphor crystallizes the extent of injustices within Micah's community, its leadership in particular, and opens eyes wide to the horrendous wickedness of which the political and community leaders are responsible.

Verse 4 presents God's response. Micah declares to the corrupted leaders that God will be unresponsive and somewhat distant from them. The notion of crying out to the Lord is a formulaic expression that occurs often in Deuteronomistic history (see, e.g., Judg 3:9, 15; 10:10). Mention of God's face being hidden from the Israelites also occurs in Ezekiel 39:23-24.

3:5-7 Proclamation concerning the prophets

Following his attack on Israel's political leadership, Micah verbally assaults Israel's prophets (3:5-7). They are guilty of leading the people astray by their false prophecies. They have corrupted their prophetic office for personal satisfaction and gain. Additionally, they respond negatively to their own Israelite audience, who fail to provide them with the expected recompense (3:5). God's response is not to punish others with physical harm

> ¹⁰Who build up Zion with blood-
> shed,
> and Jerusalem with wickedness!
> ¹¹Its leaders render judgment for a
> bribe,
> the priests teach for pay,
> the prophets divine for money,
> While they rely on the LORD,
> saying,
>
> "Is not the LORD in the midst of
> us?
> No evil can come upon us!"
> ¹²Therefore, because of you,
> Zion shall be plowed like a field,
> and Jerusalem reduced to rub-
> ble,
> And the mount of the temple
> to a forest ridge.

but to take away the gifts that are part of their prophetic office. Divine power is used to suppress rather than oppress.

Verses 5-7 have often been treated in terms of an opposition between "true" and "false" prophets. Given the context of the indictment, these prophets are not "false" prophets because they do have, according to the text, prophetic powers that God will take away from them. These prophets being addressed are true prophets who have betrayed their prophetic office and vocation.

3:8 Interlude: statement of confidence

In verse 8 the poet gives a clear picture of power as it related to the prophetic office. After two verbal attacks, Micah takes a reprieve and makes a proclamation about himself. Using the phrase "But as for me," Micah sets himself apart from those he has been attacking, namely, the political and religious leaders of Israel. He boldly states his gifts. To be "filled with power" is to be filled with God's Spirit. This first charismatic gift associates Micah with earlier figures like Saul (1 Sam 10:10; 19:23) and David, who also possessed this gift. To be filled with God's Spirit is also to be filled with justice and might. Justice is what should have been exercised by the political leaders (3:1). "Might," a term associated with military prowess (Judg 8:21), strengthens Micah so he can fearlessly hurl accusations and judgments against Israel's leaders. These gifts are divinely given, and they move the prophet to expose others' injustices to the unjust ones themselves and to those who are victims of injustice. Unlike the political and military leaders of his day whose power and might rest with the sword, Micah's power is his God-given word.

3:9-12 Address to Israel's leadership

In the last segment of Micah 1:2–3:12, Micah again attacks the political and religious leaders of his day. In verses 9-11 he launches his attack and then issues a judgment in verse 12. "Justice" (3:9) recalls 3:1 and 8. The statement that the leaders "abhor justice" reinforces the contrast between

II. Oracles of Salvation

4 ¹In days to come
the mount of the LORD's house
Shall be established as the highest
mountain;
it shall be raised above the hills,
And peoples shall stream to it:
²Many nations shall come, and
say,
"Come, let us climb the LORD's
mountain,
to the house of the God of Jacob,
That he may instruct us in his ways,
that we may walk in his paths."
For from Zion shall go forth
instruction,
and the word of the LORD from
Jerusalem.
³He shall judge between many
peoples
and set terms for strong and
distant nations;
They shall beat their swords into
plowshares,
and their spears into pruning
hooks;
One nation shall not raise the
sword against another,
nor shall they train for war again.
⁴They shall all sit under their own
vines,
under their own fig trees,
undisturbed;
for the LORD of hosts has
spoken.
⁵Though all the peoples walk,
each in the name of its god,
We will walk in the name of the
LORD,
our God, forever and ever.

the prophet and them. To his list of people, Micah adds the priest (3:11). Spiritual depravity is extensive. Finally, neither the leaders nor the holy city will escape divine retribution: justice will be served. Jerusalem and the temple will be destroyed because leadership has failed to govern with justice and integrity. Despite these harsh words, an element of hope exists. The "plowing" about to take place will be to remove the obstacles so that new seeds can be planted and can take root (cf. Jer 1:10).

PROCLAMATION OF FUTURE RESTORATION

Micah 4:1–5:14

Words of judgment now turn to words of hope and promise. Devastation will not be the final word for Israel and Judah. All that will transpire will be so that a new order, a new way of life, can be ushered in with the reign of God in the midst of all. This next section consists of a prophetic vision (4:1-5) and a divine promise (4:6–5:14).

4:1-5 Prophetic vision

The next section of the book of Micah opens with a vision of unity and peace. The poem is a prophetic vision that promises peace for the future. The vision closely parallels Isaiah 2:2-4 but stands in contrast to Micah 3:12,

⁶On that day—oracle of the LORD—
　I will gather the lame,
And I will assemble the outcasts,
　　and those whom I have afflicted.
⁷I will make of the lame a remnant,
　　and of the weak a strong nation;
The LORD shall be king over them
　　on Mount Zion,
　from now on and forever.

⁸And you, O tower of the flock,
　　hill of daughter Zion!
To you it shall come:
　　the former dominion shall be
　　　restored,
　　the reign of daughter Jerusalem.

⁹Now why do you cry out so?
　　Are you without a king?
　　Or has your adviser perished,
That you are seized with pains

like a woman in labor?
¹⁰Writhe, go into labor,
　　O daughter Zion,
　　like a woman giving birth;
For now you shall leave the city
　　and camp in the fields;
To Babylon you shall go,
　　there you shall be rescued.
There the LORD shall redeem you
　　from the hand of your enemies.

¹¹And now many nations are
　　　gathered against you!
　　They say, "Let her be profaned,
　　let our eyes see Zion's downfall!"
¹²But they do not know the
　　　thoughts of the LORD,
　　nor understand his plan:
He has gathered them
　　like sheaves to the threshing
　　　floor.

---

where both Jerusalem and the mountain of the house will be leveled. Both Micah 4:1-5 and Isaiah 2:2-4 enjoy lively conversation among scholars, and no conclusive decision has been reached about either text with regard to which one might have been more original, if borrowing has occurred, or if they are from two distinct, independent sources. Most likely the vision was a common one and perhaps part of the tradition to which both Micah and Isaiah appealed.

Although Micah addresses no particular audience here, in the context of the book of Micah as a whole the listeners would seem to be all of Israel, both the northern and southern kingdoms, and especially what would later be the faithful remnant, those once exiled, who would return to the land and through whom God's ongoing vision of world peace will evolve.

The poet begins his vision on a futuristic note, "In days to come" (4:1), and continues with a description of the mountain of the Lord's house that will be the highest of all mountains and hills. Here the poet hints at God's sovereignty, further eclipsed by the picture of all nations streaming to this mountain. Next, the poet envisions what the people who stream to the mountain will say (4:2). Israel's God will be the God of the nations. Thus, there will be one God and one people, and the house of Jacob—the "temple"—will be a house for all nations (cf. Isa 56:7; Mark 11:17). Zion, a

¹³Arise and thresh, O daughter
  Zion;
 your horn I will make iron
And your hoofs I will make bronze,
  that you may crush many
  peoples;
You shall devote their spoils to the
  LORD,

their riches to the Lord of the
  whole earth.

¹⁴Now grieve, O grieving daughter!
 "They have laid siege against
  us!"
With the rod they strike on the cheek
  the ruler of Israel.

---

city corrupted, will once again be God's dwelling place from where instruction goes forth (4:2c).

In verse 4 the poet offers a stunning portrait of God, who, as judge, does not condemn the nations but sets terms for them. Furthermore, this vision of peace would fulfill one of the Sovereign's main responsibilities, namely, to bring peace and tranquility to all nations (1 Kgs 5:5; Isa 9:7; 11:1-9; Jer 23:5-6; 33:15-16). When arbitration has taken place, when terms have been set, *then* the people will beat their swords into plowshares and their spears into pruning hooks, never again to take up the weapons of war against each other or to learn war. Micah makes clear that the way to peace is not through violence and bloodshed. In a world of peace all peoples, all nations, will enjoy world peace, and all nations, all peoples, will enjoy "the good life." Peace among nations leads to individual peace, symbolized by an agrarian image of security and stability. "Vines" and "fig trees" represent long-term stability, peace, and prosperity (4:4-5).

4:6–5:14 Divine promise

Micah 4:6-8, the opening verses of a divine promise, offers another word of hope that will occur when God draws all nations together, signaled by the phrase "On that day." This promise contrasts with Micah's present wicked days heard in Micah 1–3, with the exception of 2:12-13. These words are ironic. Those who were once the weakest among the Israelites, who endured the perversion of justice, and who are no longer under the oppression of the wicked political, social, and religious leaders of their day because these leaders will be "dethroned," will become the remnant through whom God will gather and establish a new people, a new nation, with God's reign in their midst. Whether or not the lame, scattered, and afflicted refer to the survivors of Judah during Sennacherib's invasion of Judah in 701 B.C. (cf. Isa 11:5-8) or to the Babylonian captivity is unclear and no consensus exists among scholars, though in the context of Leviticus 21:16-23, the mention of these people represents a paradigm shift and a change in Israel's thinking. These people, once prohibited from serving as priests, are now the

5 ¹But you, Bethlehem-Ephrathah
    least among the clans of Judah,
From you shall come forth for me
    one who is to be ruler in Israel;
Whose origin is from of old,
    from ancient times.
²Therefore the Lord will give them
    up, until the time
    when she who is to give birth
      has borne,
Then the rest of his kindred shall
    return
    to the children of Israel.
³He shall take his place as shepherd
    by the strength of the LORD,
    by the majestic name of the
      LORD, his God;
And they shall dwell securely, for
    now his greatness
    shall reach to the ends of the
      earth:

⁴he shall be peace.
If Assyria invades our country
    and treads upon our land,
We shall raise against it seven
    shepherds,
    eight of royal standing;
⁵They shall tend the land of Assyria
    with the sword,
    and the land of Nimrod with the
      drawn sword;
They will deliver us from Assyria,
    when it invades our land,
    when it treads upon our
      borders.

⁶The remnant of Jacob shall be
    in the midst of many peoples,
Like dew coming from the LORD,
    like showers on the grass,
Which wait for no one,
    delay for no human being.

---

recipients of God's blessing. Finally, the "tower of the flock" refers to the upper sector of the capital cities where the palace and other royal buildings stood.

In Micah 4:9-10, God, speaking through the prophet, offers a promise of deliverance. In these verses both present and future time come together. Here daughter Zion refers to Jerusalem and also personifies Jerusalem's inhabitants. The use of a rhetorical question and a simile captures the people's pain and terror, most likely from the invasion of the Babylonians into Jerusalem. The people will writhe and groan like a woman in labor because they will go into exile in Babylon. Yet, this experience will not be permanent; they will be rescued by God from the hands of their enemies (4:10). Hence, embedded in the image of a wailing woman in labor is a word of hope. Although the experience will be painful, the pain will turn to joy. Thus, at this juncture, the people are in a state of transition as they move from devastation to reprieve to restoration.

Just as Micah 4:9-10 begins with the people's present reality of calamity with the hope looming on the horizon, so too Micah 4:11-13 begins with present time, signaled by the time marker "now" (4:11; cf. 4:9). Here the poet describes an imminent attack on Jerusalem and its people (4:11). The irony is that they—the nations—are carrying out a plan designed by Israel's

⁷And the remnant of Jacob shall be
  among the nations,
    in the midst of many peoples,
  Like a lion among beasts of the
    forest,
    like a young lion among flocks
      of sheep;
  When it passes through it tramples;
    it tears and no one can rescue.
⁸Your hand shall be lifted above
    your foes,
and all your enemies shall be
  cut down.

⁹On that day—oracle of the LORD—
  I will destroy the horses from your
    midst
  and ruin your chariots;
¹⁰I will destroy the cities of your
    land
  and tear down all your
    fortresses.

God against God's only people (4:12). The twist of events comes in verse 13. Even though nations are coming to wage war against Zion, Zion will eventually prevail against them, which is also in accord with God's plan. Hence, the nations are being "set up" for defeat by Israel's God, but in the end, they will all be restored to God, together with Israel (4:1-5). Having delivered a futuristic painful yet hopeful word to Zion, the poet returns to present time, "Now" (4:14), wherein the invasion is imminent, at which time Zion will lament, "They have laid siege against us" (4:14a) as the enemies insult and slap on the face of Isaiah's ruler (4:14b). The striking of the cheek was an act of humiliation expressing contempt for a king. Thus, Israel's powerful king will be brought low.

The Israelite people, however, will not be left without a leader. The demise of a corrupt king will give way to a new leader who will come forth from Bethlehem-Ephrathah (5:1). Bethlehem was a small town five miles south of Jerusalem. David, a native of Bethlehem, was anointed there by Samuel (1 Sam 16:1-13). Ephrathah is often identified with Bethlehem (cf. Ps 136:2; Gen 35:16, 19; 48:7; 1 Sam 16:1, 18; 17:12; Ruth 4:11). The relationship between Ephrathah and Bethlehem is unclear. Ephrathah may have been the ancient name for Bethlehem, or it may have been absorbed into Bethlehem. Either way, the town was paradoxically to be the source of salvation. This new leader of Israel will be like a shepherd (Mic 5:3) and not like Israel's former kings, who used their position of authority and power to oppress the people. With this new type of governance will come security, for this new leader will be "peace" (5:4; see also Mic 5:3b; Isa 9:6-7). Hence, the poet sees a new beginning for God's people that would extend throughout the whole earth.

The remainder of verses 4-5 features Israel as the speaker; the subject is the conquest of Assyria. The reference to seven shepherds and eight leaders is a literary device used to indicate that an indefinite yet adequate number

¹¹I will destroy the sorcery you
practice,
and there shall no longer be
soothsayers among you.
¹²I will destroy your carved figures
and the sacred stones from your
midst;
And you shall no longer worship
the works of your hands.
¹³I will tear out the asherahs from
your midst,
and destroy your cities.
¹⁴I will wreak vengeance in anger
and wrath
upon the nations that have not
listened.

---

of leaders will be roused to defeat the Assyrians on Israel's behalf. The reference to "Nimrod" could refer to Babylon (Gen 10:8-9) but the parallel construction of the verse seems to indicate that the reference is to Assyria. Israel will not be defeated by either the Assyrians or the Babylonians, and the people will one day be blessed with a new just and righteous leader after all their enemies have been defeated and they—the Israelites—have returned from exile.

In Micah 5:5-8, the poet describes the faithful remnant Israel—those people who will survive the invasions and exile. The remnant itself, "[l]ike a lion among beasts of the forest" (5:7), will be victorious over its adversaries. The theme of victory introduced earlier in verse 5 is strengthened in verses 6-8.

The foreshadowed chaos that will come upon both God's people and the enemy nations that the poet proclaimed earlier now comes into full view again in Micah 5:9-14. The poet begins his proclamation with the phrase "On that day," which will not be a time of renewal and restoration (cf. 4:1). Rather, the time will be one of internal purification for Israel and the outpouring of divine wrath for the nations. As part of the messianic restoration, Israel will be stripped of everything that has caused alienation from God, including military ornament, sorcery, and idolatrous worship. The "images" were usually carved or sculptured from stone, metal, or wood. Such representations were forbidden to the Israelites (Exod 20:4; Deut 5:8). "Carved figures" refer to stone monuments with a variety of functions; they may have been symbols of the male deity (Deut 16:22; 1 Kgs 14:23). The "works of your hands" signifies idols sardonically. The "sacred stones" designate wooden cult symbols of the Canaanite mother goddess Asherah. Additionally, those nations who did not obey Israel's God would receive chastisement as well.

III. Announcement of Judgment

6 ¹Hear, then, what the LORD says:
Arise, plead your case before the
mountains,
and let the hills hear your voice!
²Hear, O mountains, the LORD's
case,
pay attention, O foundations of
the earth!
For the LORD has a case against his
people;
he enters into trial with Israel.
³My people, what have I done to
you?
how have I wearied you?
Answer me!
⁴I brought you up from the land of
Egypt,
from the place of slavery I
ransomed you;
And I sent before you Moses,
Aaron, and Miriam.
⁵My people, remember what
Moab's King Balak planned,
and how Balaam, the son of
Beor, answered him.
Recall the passage from Shittim to
Gilgal,

WORDS OF JUDGMENT, LAMENT, TRUST

Micah 6:1–7:20

The vision of all nations coming to God followed by a series of divine promises (4:1–5:14) are futuristic proclamations meant to encourage God's people as they go through the painful process of inward and outward purification before restoration can take place. Having given listeners a glimpse of what lies ahead, the poet now returns to Israel's present reality of waywardness while living under the threat of enemy invasion. Despite times of impending disaster about to befall Israel, the people remain favored by God. The poet once again reiterates God's promise of restoration to be accomplished because Israel's God is a God of compassion who remains faithful to Israel as from the days of old.

6:1-5 Covenant lawsuit

Having described the promise of Israel's glorious restoration (4:1-4, 6-8; 5:1-15), Micah once again returns to the problems plaguing Israel in present time. Verses 1-5 are cast into a *rib*, a covenant lawsuit. Micah, acting as an attorney, represents God's case against an ungrateful people. The natural elements are invoked as witnesses (6:1-2; cf. 1:2). In verses 3-5, God states the case against Israel. Instead of presenting the case in juridical language, the poet depicts God using a sorrowful and bewildered tone to confront Israel. The double use of "My people" (6:3, 5) conveys allusions to the exodus, and the plea to remember is the starting point back to right relationship. "King Balak" tried unsuccessfully to persuade the prophet Balaam to curse the Israelite armies (Num 22–24). "[F]rom Shittim to Gilgal" is from

that you may know the just
deeds of the LORD.
⁶With what shall I come before the
LORD,
and bow before God most high?
Shall I come before him with burnt
offerings,
with calves a year old?
⁷Will the LORD be pleased with
thousands of rams,
with myriad streams of oil?

Shall I give my firstborn for my
crime,
the fruit of my body for the sin
of my soul?
⁸You have been told, O mortal,
what is good,
and what the LORD requires of
you:
Only to do justice and to love
goodness,
and to walk humbly with your
God.

---

the east to the west side of the Jordan. Shittim was the site of Israel's camp under Joshua east of the Jordan River. Gilgal was the site of the Israelite camp after crossing the Jordan (Josh 3–5). The poet makes clear that God does not deserve the Israelites' lack of love, stated so movingly through the double rhetorical question that opens the passage (6:3).

6:6-8 Torah liturgy

Verses 6-8 are a response to God's questions, plea, and demand for an answer. Here Micah appears in a humbled, self-reflective, penitential state, representing his people who have yet to come before God. Micah raises four soul-searching questions aimed at atonement. Each question reflects a willingness to offer some sort of sacrifice, culminating in the offer to sacrifice one's firstborn for the sake of one's sin.

The list of sacrifices reflects Israel's ancient theological tradition. Whole burnt offerings were the typical daily offering at the temple. These offerings maintained the relationship between the Israelites and God. The suggestion of sacrificing one's own firstborn, though, raises two theological questions: (1) Was child sacrifice part of Israel's religious tradition, and (2) did Israel's God want child sacrifice as a sign of oblation?

Human sacrifice was forbidden in ancient Israel and Judah (see, e.g., Lev 18:21; 20:2-5; Deut 12:31; 18:10). In times of crisis, however, this type of sacrifice seems, on occasion, to have occurred, especially prior to the seventeenth century B.C. Human sacrifice did take place in the Canaanite religion, stemming from the god Molech and a human king who had a particular interest in this sort of sacrifice. Elsewhere in the Old Testament God expresses divine outrage at the practice of sacrificing the firstborn because they were "God's" children (Deut 32:16-19; Ezek 16:21). Hence, the reference to the sacrifice of the firstborn is more hyperbolic and metaphorical than actual. Whether or not such a sacrifice would be pleasing to God

⁹The LORD cries aloud to the city
(It is prudent to fear your
name!):
Hear, O tribe and city assembly,
¹⁰Am I to bear criminal hoarding
and the accursed short ephah?
¹¹Shall I acquit crooked scales,
bags of false weights?
¹²You whose wealthy are full of
violence,
whose inhabitants speak falsehood
with deceitful tongues in their
mouths!
¹³I have begun to strike you
with devastation because of
your sins.
¹⁴You shall eat, without being
satisfied,
food that will leave you empty;

and suffice for atonement comes clear in verse 8. What God requires is for one to do justice, love kindness, and walk humbly with God. The last is the most important one. Only when one takes a humble walk with God will one come to learn and understand how to do justice and love kindness.

Theologically, justice is identified with the nature of God (Isa 30:18) and is an activity of God (Gen 18:25; Ps 9:5). Justice is a transformative virtue that seeks to establish or restore community while aiming to balance personal good with the common good. Three types of justice include (1) commutative justice that focuses on relationships between members of the community; (2) distributive justice that functions to ensure the equitable distribution of goods, benefits, and burdens of a community; and (3) social justice that affects the social order necessary for distributive justice. To love kindness involves both affection and ethical love of neighbor and fidelity to covenant and law. To walk humbly with God implies an attitude of reverence and openness coupled with a sense of personal integrity, candidness, and honesty. God's people are called to godliness and to live out the fullness of justice and love.

Finally, the early church fathers have interpreted Micah 6:1-8 in a variety of ways. Cyril emphasizes God's compassion. Tertullian states that God expects people to act with the same divine mercy and compassion that have been bestowed upon them. Both Theodore of Mopsuestia and Augustine note that the love of God, the love of neighbor, and the offering of self in loving service to one another is far superior to any other sacrifice or burnt offering.

6:9-16 Judgment speech

God's tone changes in verses 9-16. No longer sad and bewildered, Israel's God now indicts the wicked ones among the Israelites in Jerusalem because of their social sins (6:9-12) and then casts judgment upon this wayward people (6:13-16). In verses 1-2, the mountains and hills were called to listen to God's case against the people; now Jerusalem and its inhabitants

What you acquire, you cannot save;
    what you do save, I will deliver
      up to the sword.
¹⁵You shall sow, yet not reap,
    tread out the olive, yet pour no
      oil,
    crush the grapes, yet drink no
      wine.
¹⁶You have kept the decrees of Omri,

and all the works of the house of
    Ahab,
and you have walked in their
    counsels;
Therefore I will deliver you up to
    ruin,
and your citizens to derision;
and you shall bear the reproach
    of the nations.

---

are called to listen to what God has to say (6:9). The divine indictment against the people begins in verses 10-11 with a double rhetorical question that highlights God's intolerance for injustice. The charge is for cheating done with fraudulent weights and measures (Lev 19:35-36; Deut 25:13-16). God will deliver the people from their external enemies, but God will not deliver the people from themselves and their own crimes (6:13).

In verses 14-15 the poet uses a series of five statements to outline the hardships that many of the people will have to endure because of their own wickedness. All of their efforts at trying to feed and sustain themselves will be futile. These curses invoked on the people as a response to their unjust ways are based on the old covenant curses. The first statement reflects Leviticus 26:26b; the second contains overtones of Deuteronomy 28:47-57; the third recalls Leviticus 26:16 and Deuteronomy 28:38; and the fourth corresponds to Deuteronomy 28:40. All of these curses reflect the typical forms of cursing statements found in ancient Near Eastern treaty texts.

Verse 16 is a further indictment against the inhabitants of Jerusalem. Here the poet alludes to two of Israel's wicked kings whose ways the people of Jerusalem have followed. Omri and Ahab were two infamous kings of Samaria who ruled from around 885–850 B.C. Omri was the sixth king of the northern kingdom Israel. He had once commanded Israel's army under King Elah. After a series of events, Omri became king and ruled wickedly. Ahab was Omri's son and successor. The seventh king of Israel (1 Kgs 16:30), he was influenced by his wife Jezebel, who worshiped Baal (1 Kgs 16:31-34; 18). Thus, Ahab gave Baal equal place with God. Ahab also built a temple to Baal in which he erected a wooden image of the Canaanite goddess Asherah (1 Kgs 16:33). Urged by Jezebel, Ahab opposed the worship of God, and killed all God's prophets. He ruled over Israel in Samaria for twenty-two years, from 873–852 B.C. (1 Kgs 16:29). Ahab's loss of right relationship with God led to immoral civil acts, the most famous of which is the takeover of Naboth's vineyard. The heinous deed was done through conspiracy and murder. Ahab murdered Naboth in order to claim his land in

7 ¹Woe is me! I am like the one who gathers summer fruit,
when the vines have been gleaned;
There is no cluster to eat,
no early fig that I crave.
²The faithful have vanished from the earth,
no mortal is just!
They all lie in wait to shed blood,
each one ensnares the other.
³Their hands succeed at evil;
the prince makes demands,
The judge is bought for a price,
the powerful speak as they please.
⁴The best of them is like a brier,
the most honest like a thorn hedge.
The day announced by your sentinels!
Your punishment has come;
now is the time of your confusion.
⁵Put no faith in a friend,
do not trust a companion;
With her who lies in your embrace
watch what you say.
⁶For the son belittles his father,
the daughter rises up against her mother,
The daughter-in-law against her mother-in-law,
and your enemies are members of your household.

---

the Jezreel Valley (1 Kgs 21). The prophet Elijah opposed Ahab, and through Elijah the wrath of God came down upon Ahab (1 Kgs 21–22). Both Omri and Ahab were guilty of syncretism and apostasy (1 Kgs 16:25-26, 30-33).

In verse 16 the people of Jerusalem stand indicted by their God because they have followed the wicked ways of wicked kings instead of following God and God's ways. Such wickedness led to the demise of the northern kingdom Israel, and these same transgressions of syncretism and idolatry will lead to the demise of the southern kingdom Judah. The inhabitants of Jerusalem and all of Judah will be delivered up to ruin and will become objects of scorn and mockery among the nations (6:16b). Thus, God's people will have to bear the consequences of their own sinfulness.

7:1-6 Lament

Micah 7:1-6 is a poignant lament spoken by the prophet Micah, who feels alone and abandoned as he undertakes the futile task of trying to find one upright person in the land. Abraham before him tried to do the same task (Gen 18:23-33), and Jeremiah and Ezekiel after him also tried to do the same thing (Jer 5:1-5; Ezek 22:30, respectively). In the midst of his dreadful situation, however, the prophet never loses faith and hope in God (7:7). A series of vivid images captures Micah's desperation. His lament begins with a wail—"Woe is me!"—for he sees no one righteous in the land and he finds himself among the violently wicked, the only ones remaining in the land. The summer fruit and the vintage are some of the last crops to be gathered at the end of the harvest season during the late summer and early fall, just before the festival Sukkoth (Tabernacles) takes place, which marks

IV. Confidence in God's Future

⁷But as for me, I will look to the
    LORD,
  I will wait for God my savior;
    my God will hear me!
⁸Do not rejoice over me, my enemy!
    though I have fallen, I will arise;
    though I sit in darkness, the
      LORD is my light.

⁹I will endure the wrath of the LORD
    because I have sinned against
      him,
Until he pleads my case,
    and establishes my right.
He will bring me forth to the light;
    I will see his righteousness.
¹⁰When my enemy sees this,
    shame shall cover her:

---

the conclusion of the fruit harvest and the start of the rainy season. Taking the persona of one who goes out into the orchard after the summer fruit has been picked or into the vineyard after the grapes have been gathered, hoping to find some good fruit, Micah complains that just as no clusters or early figs remain, so the "faithful have vanished from the earth" (7:1-2). The only ones remaining in the land are murderers, predators, and thieves who act like animals hunting for their prey (7:2).

Verse 3 recalls Micah 3:11, which speaks of Israel's leaders taking bribes. Corruption runs rampant, beginning with the hierarchy. Those in power assert their power for their own selfish and self-serving interests. No justice exists for those who have little or no money since judges are bought for a price and render judgments for a bribe. These offenses are similar to those heard in Micah 2:2, 8-9; 3:9-11. No honesty and integrity exists in the land. To those who have corrupted their office and have caused pain to others, punishment will be meted out (7:4).

Political and social depravity has led to the breakdown of community and family (7:5-6). Here Micah issues a warning not to trust in friends, companions, or family members because in the depraved state of the land, people turn on one another. In ancient times, betrayal of family members by other family members is a serious situation because the family was a stabilizing and integrating structure within the Israelite society. The cohesiveness of the family structure and hence the society depended on the absolute authority of paterfamilias and the respect of his children for him and his spouse. Included in the family circle are daughters-in-law because they leave their own families, become attached to their husbands, and remain subject to their husbands' fathers. Thus, human relationship has become sick at the core and no longer functions properly, particularly because of the lack of trust.

7:7-10 Statement of trust

Having expressed the lack of trust that exists among the family and community members (7:6), Micah now utters a word of hope. The phrase

She who said to me,
   "Where is the LORD, your God?"
My eyes shall see her downfall;
   now she will be trampled
      underfoot,
   like mud in the streets.
[11]It is the day for building your walls;
   on that day your boundaries
      shall be enlarged.

[12]It is the day when those from
      Assyria to Egypt
   shall come to you,
And from Tyre even to the River,
   from sea to sea, and from
      mountain to mountain;
[13]And the earth shall be a waste
   because of its inhabitants,
   as a result of their deeds.

"But as for me" (7:7) is a *casus pendens*. It functions to separate Micah from the rest of his dishonorable community members. Having been disappointed by the human condition, Micah places his hope in God. With confidence he will wait for his God who is his salvation. This God will hear him and respond to him just as God has done in the past for Micah's ancestors (Exod 2:24-25; 3:7-10). The triple reference to God attests to Micah's faith. The prophet's statement of trust and confidence in God becomes a lesson and a word of hope for the faithful remnant of the Israelite community, who, for a time, will have to suffer pain and exile.

In verses 8-10 Micah speaks on behalf of his community, who, confident of its deliverance, confesses its transgressions. Assurance in God heard in verse 7 continues in verse 8. The one who will become the taunt of nations (2:4) will be the one to rise in future days, but for now both the prophet and the people will have to bear God's indignation for having sinned. God's indignation refers to all the horror, trauma, calamity, and destruction that will befall the northern kingdom Israel and the southern kingdom Judah. The invasion and collapse of these two kingdoms was inevitable historically, but the prophet sees the demise of the two kingdoms as divinely imposed consequences for sin. The text reflects the community's belief in the Deuteronomistic theory of retribution (see Deut 28). This suffering, however, will have to be endured only for a time because God will vindicate the one being chastised, and those enemies who stand in judgment with mockery and scorn will be put to shame (7:9-10). Finally, verses 8-10 provide a window into the office and vocation of the prophet who is called to make intercession for transgressors, which sometimes entails bearing the pain of not only a community's sin but also the anger and sadness of God at a people who have forsaken God and God's ways.

7:11-13 Divine promise

Words of lament with glimmers of hope interspersed (7:8-10) turn to words of excitement in a vision that describes future restoration and re-

¹⁴Shepherd your people with your
staff,
the flock of your heritage,
That lives apart in a woodland,
in the midst of an orchard.
Let them feed in Bashan and Gilead,
as in the days of old;
¹⁵As in the days when you came
from the land of Egypt,
show us wonderful signs.
¹⁶The nations will see and will be
put to shame,
in spite of all their strength;
They will put their hands over their
mouths;
their ears will become deaf.
¹⁷They will lick the dust like a
snake,
like crawling things on the
ground;
They will come quaking from their
strongholds;
they will tremble in fear of you,
the LORD, our God.

population. Addressed to Jerusalem, the city has endured divine judgment and, as a result of this judgment, has suffered greatly. Now Jerusalem is promised restoration. Here the poet speaks as if the time of restoration is imminent: "It is the day for building your walls" (7:11). When this day dawns, Jerusalem's boundaries will also be enlarged, allowing for two superpower nations, Assyria and Egypt, as well as others, to come to it from near and far. With expanded boundaries, Jerusalem will be the gathering place of the nations, a theme echoed in Micah 4:1-4. This restoration and repopulation will be gradual. The earth itself will be a waste because of the peoples' deeds. Restoration and renewal is a gradual process.

The reference to "the River" (7:12) pertains to the Euphrates River of Mesopotamia (cf. Gen 15:18; Deut 1:7; Josh 1:4; 2 Sam 8:3; 1 Chr 18:3). This reference plays upon Israel's traditional boundaries, which would have extended from the Euphrates to Egypt (Gen 15:18; Num 34; 2 Sam 8; Ezek 47:13-20).

7:14-17 Petition

Words of promise shift to words of petition. Here the poet portrays Micah petitioning God to shepherd the people of Israel and to let them graze in the finest of pastures. The plea to have God act as a shepherd recalls an earlier shepherd metaphor in Micah 2:12-13. There Micah assures the people that God will gather the remnant and lead them out of exile (cf. 4:6-10). Now Micah wants God to lead the people into restoration (cf. 5:4). "Bashan" refers to the plains southwest of Syria that overlook the Sea of Galilee; "Gilead" is the Israelite region of the Transjordan south of the Sea of Galilee and north of the Dead Sea. Both areas are excellent for grazing (cf. Num 32:1; Ps 22:12; Amos 4:1; Ezek 27:6; Song 6:5). Jerusalem and Judah's restoration will astound the nations, and they will stand in humiliation and awe at the power of Israel's God.

¹⁸Who is a God like you, who
removes guilt
and pardons sin for the remnant
of his inheritance;
Who does not persist in anger
forever,
but instead delights in mercy,
¹⁹And will again have compassion
on us,
treading underfoot our
iniquities?
You will cast into the depths of the
sea all our sins;
²⁰You will show faithfulness to
Jacob,
and loyalty to Abraham,
As you have sworn to our ancestors
from days of old.

7:18-20 Statement of divine love

The poet closes the book of Micah with a word of praise. On behalf of the community, Micah makes a heartfelt confession of faith that acknowledges the true essence of who God is. Israel's God is, ultimately, a God of forgiveness and compassion whose anger is only a passing emotion. This God remains faithful to covenant (Gen 12; 15; 17; 28; 35) and faithful to the people. Here the poet's words echo Exodus 34:6-7. Judgment, destruction, and annihilation are never the final words of God. The final word and work is always forgiveness, always compassion, as Israel's God works continually to restore and transform both the human condition and all of creation.

Nahum

With frightful and gruesome images, the prophet Nahum delivers a stinging message to the Assyrian leaders and people and, in particular, to Nineveh, Assyria's capital city. Israel's warrior God is about to destroy Nineveh, the "bloody city" full of lies and plunder "whose looting never stops!" (3:1). A "multitude of slain, / a mass of corpses, / Endless bodies / to stumble upon" will be all that remains (3:3). This message is a harrowing one for Nineveh and Assyria but good news for Judah. Judah's enemy will be squelched, never to rise again. Indeed, for Judah, this impending catastrophic event will be a time of celebration, a time for renewing covenant bonds with God, and a time for long-awaited peace (2:1). The warfare imagery used throughout the book foreshadows the invasion of the Babylonians and Persians who eventually sacked Nineveh. According to the text, this combined assault on Nineveh was in keeping with God's divine intention and orchestrated by God as well. The Assyrians, a people greatly feared in the region, are about to encounter one greater and more powerful than themselves. They are about to experience Israel's God, who will work through the Babylonians and the Medes to accomplish justice for Judah.

The world of Nahum

The book of Nahum offers a word of peril to Assyria and particularly to Nineveh and its inhabitants, and a word of hope and consolation to Judah, who has long endured the injustices and oppression of Assyria, Judah's enemy nation. Historically, Assyria ruled by brute force and gained power in the region by exacting heavy tributes, deporting entire populations of people, and permitting no compromise or repudiation of treaties. Assyria became known as the lion of the ancient Near East. Assyria's leaders were fearless. Tiglath-pileser III (745–727 B.C.) conquered Israel; Sargon II (721–705 B.C.) and Sennacherib (705–681 B.C.) made Judah a vassal state; and Ashurbanipal (668–627 B.C.) devastated Thebes in Egypt and burned Babylon. When Ashurbanipal died in 627 B.C., coalitions of Medes and Babylonians sought revenge against Assyria. In 612 B.C. the armies of these countries took

105

The prophet Nahum, sculpted by Aleijadinho, in front of the church of the Sanctuary of Bom Jesus of Matosinhos at Congonhas, Minas Gerais, Brazil.

Nineveh by force and destroyed it. With the destruction of Nineveh came the eventual collapse of the Assyrian Empire, and, remarkably, its rise and fall happened in less than a century and a half. The general consensus among scholars is that Nahum was active as a prophet while Ashurbanipal was reigning, since Nahum 1:12 describes the Assyrians and Nineveh "fully intact and so numerous." During this time, Judah was quite possibly experiencing a period of reform, since Nahum's words allude to Judah having been humbled by God who is now going to liberate the people from their oppressive bonds (1:13). Finally, little is known about Nahum himself, and, like the other prophets mentioned in the Bible's collection of Prophetic Books, whether or not Nahum was an actual historical person continues to be a topic of debate among biblical scholars.

The literary dimensions of the book of Nahum

Perhaps no other book among the prophets has such graphic imagery as the text of Nahum. These images have one single focus and reflect one single purpose: a war about to be waged against Judah's ferocious enemy. Most of these images reflect the culture of the day and life on the battlefield. Some images are drawn from the natual world and used metaphorically to emphasize the force and strength of Israel's God over the Assyrians and, specifically, the inhabitants of Nineveh. Israel's God will be like a lion (2:12), and all of the enemy's fortresses, like fig trees with first-ripe figs, will "fall / into the devourer's mouth" when these fig-tree-like fortresses are shaken (3:12). One of the other striking elements in the book of Nahum is the use of foreshadowing. Through Nahum's prophetic vision, the poet vividly portrays what is about to befall Assyria and Nineveh. Although the book's imagery is effective in establishing its central message, one cannot overlook the inherent violence in the text's images and metaphors. Those images and metaphors are gender specific, as in the case of Nahum 3:5-7, where female imagery is used to describe Nineveh's forthcoming humiliation. Indeed, the prophet is the bearer of good news for Judah, but the poetry, in general, is difficult to hear because its celebratory tone comes at the expense of the complete devastation of another, a scenario that continues to plague contemporary times in search for peace and the transformation of religious imagination.

The book of Nahum can be divided into the following divisions and subdivisions:

I. Superscription (1:1)
II. A hymn to God (1:2-11)

III. A word of good news to Judah (1:12–2:1)
IV. A prophetic vision concerning Nineveh (2:2–3:19)
   Proclamation of an impending divine attack against Nineveh (2:2-14)
   Proclamation against Nineveh (3:1-17)
   Proclamation against the king of Assyria (3:18-19)

Each division and subdivision features an array of literary techniques, in addition to imagery, metaphors, similes, and foreshadowing. The poet is adept at using personification (1:5) and rhetorical questions (1:6; 3:8, 19), and, like many of the other poets of the Prophetic Books, the poet Nahum presents God anthropomorphically and anthropocentrically. Israel's God is like the warriors of old, but warrior God is more powerful than all the human and nonhuman powers on earth. The poet also depicts God as a storm God and a king. All of these techniques contribute to the overall theological message of the book of Nahum, which is that Israel's God does not and will not tolerate injustice.

The theological dimensions of the book of Nahum

For years, Assyria has oppressed kingdoms and countries, Israel and Judah included. Nahum's audience now learns, in gritty detail, that just as Assyria made others suffer, so now Assyria will be made to suffer: Nineveh will be destroyed. In some respects, the portrait of justice depicted in the book of Nahum reflects the old adage "What goes around, comes around." The tone is somber for the Assyrians and Ninevites but jubilant for the Judahites. The "holy war" about to take place will be liberating for those who have long suffered oppression, but this liberation will come at the cost of human life. History has borne out that liberation through violence does not bring lasting peace. Thus, the book of Nahum is about justice, but the way that such justice is achieved invites further critical theological reflection and comment.

Nahum

1 ¹Oracle concerning Nineveh. The book of the vision of Nahum of Elkosh.

God's Terrifying Appearance

²A jealous and avenging God is the LORD,
an avenger is the LORD, full of wrath;
The LORD takes vengeance on his adversaries,
and rages against his enemies;
³The LORD is slow to anger, yet great in power;
the LORD will not leave the guilty unpunished.
In stormwind and tempest he comes,
and clouds are the dust at his feet;

⁴He roars at the sea and leaves it dry,
and all the rivers he dries up.
Laid low are Bashan and Carmel,
and the bloom of Lebanon withers;
⁵The mountains quake before him,
and the hills dissolve;
The earth is laid waste before him,
the world and all who dwell in it.
⁶Before his wrath, who can stand firm,
and who can face his blazing anger?
His fury is poured out like fire,
and boulders break apart before him.

SUPERSCRIPTION

Nahum 1:1

Verse 1 sets the stage for Nahum's proclamations: they are addressed to Nineveh, the capital of Assyria. The prophet's message is the result of a divine vision, one that was undoubtedly an intuitive experience. The location of Elkosh is unknown. Nahum's name means "the one consoled."

A HYMN TO GOD

Nahum 1:2-11

One of the most vivid and horrifying pictures of the God of justice appears in Nahum 1:2-11. Without reservation, Nahum proclaims that God is about to act on Judah's behalf but to the demise of the Assyrians. This God

⁷The LORD is good to those who
   wait for him,
a refuge on the day of distress,
Taking care of those who look to
   him for protection,
⁸when the flood rages;
He makes an end of his opponents,
   and pursues his enemies into
   darkness.

Nineveh's Judgment and Judah's Restoration

⁹What do you plot against the
   LORD,
the one about to bring total
   destruction?
No opponent rises a second time!

¹⁰Like a thorny thicket, they are tan-
   gled,
and like drunkards, they are
   drunk;
like dry stubble, they are utterly
   consumed.
¹¹From you has come
one plotting evil against the
   LORD,
one giving sinister counsel.
¹²Thus says the LORD:
though fully intact and so
   numerous,
they shall be mown down and
   disappear.
Though I have humbled you,
I will humble you no more.

---

is a "jealous and avenging God," one who is "full of wrath," who "takes vengeance on his adversaries" (1:2), and who does not clear the guilty (1:3). This God is the storm God who rebukes the sea, dries up all the rivers, and makes the flowers die, the mountains quake, the hills melt, and the earth heave (1:3-5). Bashan (1:4), the district east of Jordan and north of Gilead, was rich in grain and known for its breed of cattle. Carmel (1:4) was a 1,742-feet-high hill associated with the history of Elijah and Elisha (1 Kgs 18; 2 Kgs 2:25; 4:25). Lebanon (1:4) was a long range of hills that rose to about eight or nine thousand feet in the extreme north of Palestine and was known as the land of forests with groves of cedars. Nahum makes clear that divine protection is extended to those who take refuge in God, but God will make a full end of the adversaries and will pursue the enemies (1:8). With this proclamation, Nahum warns the Assyrians and those in Nineveh about Israel's God, who is stronger and more ferocious than the best of the military and political leaders. Those who have plotted and done evil against Israel's God and Israel are about to receive the same treatment (1:11). Nahum's rhetorical question in verse 9 and similes in verse 10 seal Nineveh's fate.

A WORD OF GOOD NEWS TO JUDAH

Nahum 1:12–2:1

With gusto, Nahum proclaims a word of hope to the inhabitants of Judah, announcing the end of their affliction by the Assyrians. The yoke bonds that have bound the country for years are about to be broken. Historically, these

¹³Now I will break his yoke off of
you,
and tear off your bonds.

¹⁴The LORD has commanded
regarding you:
no descendant will again bear
your name;
From the house of your gods I will
abolish
the carved and the molten
image;
I will make your grave a dung
heap.

2 ¹At this moment on the mountains
the footsteps of one bearing
good news,
of one announcing peace!
Celebrate your feasts, Judah,
fulfill your vows!
For never again will destroyers
invade you;
they are completely cut off.

The Attack on Nineveh

²One who scatters has come up
against you;
guard the rampart,

---

verses refer to the conflict between Assyria and Judah (see 1:1). For more than three hundred years, Assyria had controlled the Near Eastern world, including Judah. The Judahites had thought that God had sent the Assyrians against them as a way to chastise them for their apostasy and wickedness. Here the poet depicts God promising to end such affliction. God will now assert divine power for the sake of liberation (1:12-13). The God who once caused Judah to be overpowered now promises to end its distress.

Verse 14 addresses the king of Assyria. To liberate the Judahites, God now promises to destroy the Assyrian ruler, Ashurbanipal, his lineage, and his gods. The Assyrians and their king will be humiliated; their trusted gods will come to naught.

In Nahum 2:1 the prophet exhorts Judah to rejoice. Written in present tense, the poem anticipates the end of Assyrian captivity. The festivals to be celebrated probably are the Passover meal, Pentecost, and Booths that commemorate salvation, liberation, redemption, and a plentiful harvest, respectively. Judah will then be able to celebrate its festivals and fulfill the pledges it has made to God. This, Nahum 1:12–2:1, celebrates the end of Assyrian oppression, an event that Nahum 2 and 3 describe in detail.

A PROPHETIC VISION CONCERNING NINEVEH

Nahum 2:2–3:19

This next section describes the attack on and downfall of Nineveh (2:2–3:17). It also features a proclamation against Assyria's king (3:18-19). With graphic detail, the prophet gives an account of what the battle against Nineveh will entail. The proclamation is futuristic; yet the poet's use of

Watch the road, brace yourselves,
   marshal all your strength!
³The LORD will restore the vine of
   Jacob,
   the honor of Israel,
Because ravagers have ravaged
   them
   and ruined their branches.
⁴The shields of his warriors are
   crimsoned,
   the soldiers clad in scarlet;
Like fire are the trappings of the
   chariots
   on the day he prepares for war;
   the cavalry is agitated!
⁵The chariots dash madly through
   the streets
   and wheel in the squares,
Looking like torches,
   bolting like lightning.
⁶His picked troops are called,
   ranks break at their charge;
To the wall they rush,
   their screen is set up.
⁷The river gates are opened,

the palace is washed away.
⁸The mistress is led forth captive,
   and her maidservants led away,
Moaning like doves,
   beating their breasts.
⁹Nineveh is like a pool
   whose waters escape;
"Stop! Stop!"
   but none turns back.
¹⁰"Plunder the silver, plunder the
   gold!"
   There is no end to the treasure,
   to wealth in every precious
   thing!

¹¹Emptiness, desolation, waste;
   melting hearts and trembling
   knees,
Churning in every stomach,
   every face turning pale!
¹²Where is the lionesses' den,
   the young lions' cave,
Where the lion went in and out,
   and the cub, with no one to
   disturb them?

---

present tense verbs throughout it functions as an assurance to the people of Judah that, indeed, what has been foreseen by Nahum will come to pass.

2:2-14 Proclamation of an impending divine attack against Nineveh

In verse 2 the prophet issues a warning to the Ninevites: they are to prepare for battle. Four rapid-fire imperatives, "guard," "watch," "brace," and "marshal," alert them to be on the defensive. In verse 3 Nahum reveals to this enemy nation who their opponent will be and why they are about to be challenged. Israel's God is about to stop the oppression being done to Judah by the Assyrians, who are indirectly referred to as "ravagers."

Verses 4-14 describe God's warriors and the imminent attack on Nineveh. The warriors will be the Babylonians and the Medes, who, according to the text, will be the warriors God will use to defeat the Ninevites and, essentially, the Assyrian Empire. The crimson shields represent the battle stains from past victories. The soldiers' scarlet uniforms symbolize the brilliance and boldness of the army ready for war. Verse 5 commences the battle: the chariots—the vehicles of devastation—race full force into Nineveh.

¹³The lion tore apart enough for his
    cubs,
    and strangled for his lionesses;
He filled his lairs with prey,
    and his dens with torn flesh.
¹⁴I now come against you—
    oracle of the Lord of hosts—
I will consume your chariots in
    smoke,
    and the sword will devour your
    young lions;

Your preying on the land I will
    bring to an end,
    the cry of your lionesses will be
    heard no more.

3 ¹Ah! The bloody city,
    all lies,
Full of plunder,
    whose looting never stops!
²The crack of the whip,
    the rumbling of wheels;
Horses galloping,
    chariots bounding,

Verses 6-11 describe the siege and destruction of Nineveh. A variety of similes and metaphors create a graphic picture of a once fearsome people now taken captive, moaning like doves, and beating their breasts. In verse 8 the "mistress" refers to Nineveh itself, and the "maidservants" is a reference to Nineveh's inhabitants. This invasion of Nineveh will be relentless (2:9), leaving the city devastated and its peoples completely plundered and trembling (2:10-11). A city and a people once so feared have received from another the same kind of treatment that they have done to others for years. Using metaphorical language from the natural world, the poet next features Nahum mocking the false strength of Nineveh (2:12-14), symbolized by the reference to lions. In the Old Testament, the lion evokes ferocity, destructive power, and irresistible strength. It is sometimes described as a bold and valiant warrior (Prov 28:1; 30:30). Lions also symbolize the power of royalty. In verses 12-14 the den of lions pertains to the royalty of Nineveh—its kings, queens, and princes who exert brute force.

Verse 14 shifts to actual present time. Having proclaimed the vision of the destruction of Nineveh, Nahum now delivers another word from God: "I now come against you" (2:14a). The invasion is imminent. Nineveh will soon meet the "lion" of Judah (cf. Jer 49:19; Hos 11:10; 13:7-8), and what has been foreshadowed in verses 6-11 will surely happen. Nineveh's royalty and all its inhabitants, symbolized by the reference to "young lions," will meet their demise (2:14bc). Israel's God takes full responsibility for the plans, and, by accepting full responsibility, Israel's God asserts divine sovereignty over the strongest of nations. Justice will be meted out punitively, an action that reflects the culture and people's belief in *lex talionis*. LAW OF RETALIATION

3:1-17 Proclamation against Nineveh

This next section describes further what is about to befall Nineveh. The material is similar to Nahum 2:2, 4-11, but now the images are much more

³Cavalry charging,
   the flash of the sword,
   the gleam of the spear;
A multitude of slain,
   a mass of corpses,
Endless bodies
   to stumble upon!
⁴For the many debaucheries of the
      prostitute,
   a charming mistress of witchcraft,
Who enslaved nations with her
      prostitution,
   and peoples by her witchcraft:
⁵I now come against you—
   oracle of the LORD of hosts—
   and I will lift your skirt above
      your face;
I will show your nakedness to the
      nations,
   to the kingdoms your shame!
⁶I will cast filth upon you,
   disgrace you and make you a
      spectacle;

⁷Until everyone who sees you
   runs from you saying,
"Nineveh is destroyed;
   who can pity her?
Where can I find
   any to console you?"

Nineveh's Inescapable Fate

⁸Are you better than No-amon
   that was set among the Nile's
      canals,
Surrounded by waters,
   with the river for her rampart
   and water for her wall?
⁹Ethiopia was her strength,
   and Egypt without end;
Put and the Libyans
   were her allies.
¹⁰Yet even she became an exile,
   and went into captivity;
Even her little ones were dashed to
      pieces
   at the corner of every street;

gruesome and include blood, lies, plunder, harlotries, corpses, filth, and sorceries. With respect to imagery, verse 5 presents the most repulsive image not only because of its description but also because it is gender-specific and thus troublesome because of its female reference. The same is true for verse 13 that compares Nineveh's troops to women. The metaphor succeeds in its intent to mock Nineveh, but it remains offensive to women, who are being imaged as weaker than men. Verse 5 echoes 2:14; the destruction of Nineveh draws even closer.

Verses 8-13 begin with an interrogation and contain a variety of metaphors. The prophet reminds Nineveh that No-amon (Thebes), the capital of Egypt and Nineveh's major rival, was devastated despite the city's many natural advantages. Nineveh is no better than Thebes and will suffer the same consequence—destruction, most explicitly captured by the phrase "Even her little ones were dashed to pieces / at the corner of every street" (3:10b). Just as Nineveh's figs are ready to be picked, so the city's fortifications are ripe for the taking (3:12). Just as a swarm of locusts vanish when the sun rises, so the multitudes of Assyrian officials will soon disappear under the heat of invasion (3:17).

For her nobles they cast lots,
  and all her great ones were put
    into chains.
[11]You, too, will drink of this;
  you will be overcome;
You, too, will seek
  a refuge from the foe.
[12]But all your fortresses are fig trees,
  bearing early figs;
When shaken, they fall
  into the devourer's mouth.
[13]Indeed your troops
  are women in your midst;
To your foes are open wide
  the gates of your land,
  fire has consumed their bars.
[14]Draw water for the siege,
  strengthen your fortresses;
Go down into the mud
  and tread the clay,
  take hold of the brick mold!
[15]There the fire will consume you,
  the sword will cut you down;
  it will consume you like the
    grasshoppers.

Multiply like the grasshoppers,

multiply like the locusts!
[16]You have made your traders more
    numerous
  than the stars of the heavens;
  like grasshoppers that shed their
    skins and fly away.
[17]Your sentries are like locusts,
  and your scribes like locust
    swarms
Gathered on the rubble fences
  on a cold day!
Yet when the sun rises, they vanish,
  and no one knows where they
    have gone.

[18]Your shepherds slumber,
  O king of Assyria,
  your nobles have gone to rest;
Your people are scattered upon the
    mountains,
  with none to gather them.
[19]There is no healing for your hurt,
  your wound is fatal.
All who hear this news of you
  clap their hands over you;
For who has not suffered
  under your endless malice?

3:18-19 Proclamation against the king of Assyria

The focus shifts from Nineveh and the Assyrian officials to the Assyrian king. The imagery denotes not only the ineffectiveness of the king's leaders but also the king himself, which has led to the dissolution of his people. Ultimately, the king has failed at governing well, which leaves open the door for the impending siege. The poem closes on a note of jubilation for Judah: Judah's oppressor will now be oppressed.

Zephaniah

Zephaniah was a contemporary of Nahum and Habakkuk, and, like his contemporaries, Zephaniah preached during the Babylonian crisis prior to the fall of Jerusalem in 587 B.C. Like many prophets of his time, very little is known about his background and if, in fact, he was an actual historical figure. The message that Zephaniah delivers is a harrowing one that forewarns about the coming judgment upon Judah (1:1-13), the great Day of the Lord (1:14-18), and judgment on Israel's enemies (2:1-15). Zephaniah also describes the wickedness of Jerusalem (3:1-7) and God's intentions to chastise and transform the nations (3:1-13). He concludes his proclamation with a song of joy (3:14-20) to be sung with gusto because Jerusalem will be restored (3:20). The tone of this prophetic book is foreboding yet hopeful, and, like so many of the other prophetic texts, Zephaniah has its share of violent images that reflect the times and culture of the day. The book is fast-paced and celebrates a God who will not tolerate injustice and transgression, namely, Judah's worship of other gods (1:4-9) and its unjust and abusive leadership (3:1-4).

The world of Zephaniah

The book of Zephaniah opens with a superscription (1:1) that links the prophet Zephaniah to the period when King Josiah reigned (640–609 B.C.). Interestingly, a period of silence existed in the Old Testament prophets, specifically during the first three quarters of the seventh century B.C. (698–626 B.C.). One possibility for the silence was because of Judah's kings—Manasseh (686–642 B.C.) and Amon (642–640 B.C.)—who were being controlled by the Assyrians and supposedly by the Assyrians' gods. Manasseh's reign was during the zenith of Assyria's power. On the home front, Judah was guilty of ever-increasing persecution, idolatry, and child-sacrifice (2 Kgs 21:1-9, 16).

With respect to Assyria, Sennacherib (705–681 B.C.), one of Assyria's greatest kings, was murdered in 681 B.C. His successor was his son, Esarhaddon (680–669 B.C.), a strong king who extended Assyria's empire as far west

as Egypt, which occurred when he captured Memphis in 671 B.C. Esarhaddon's successor was Ashurbanipal (668–627 B.C.). He strengthened Assyria's stronghold on Egypt by conquering Thebes in 663 B.C. After the death of Ashurbanipal around 627 B.C., Assyria's power weakened considerably, which opened the door for Josiah's reforms in Judah, beginning in 621 B.C. Assyria's decline in power also paved the way for the Babylonians to rise to world power under the leadership of Nabopolassar (625–605 B.C.) and Nebuchadnezzar (605–562 B.C.). The text of Zephaniah reflects the Assyrian period and the life of Judah at that time.

The literary dimensions of the book of Zephaniah

The book of Zephaniah moves at a rapid pace. A variety of images, descriptions, and metaphors keep readers enwrapped in God's fury. The repetitious use of the phrase "on that day" and its related references (see 1:9, 10, 14-16, 18; 2:1; 3:11) add cohesion to the series of prophecies of destruction while providing an element of surprise: the Day of the Lord is a time of destruction (1:9-10) that will give way to a time of cleansing and restoration (3:11-13). Throughout the book, the poet also uses the technique of cataloguing—"I will . . ." (1:2-4, 8-9, 12, 17; 3:9-12, 18-20)—to emphasize the power and deeds of Israel's God. The use of quoted speech (1:12; 2:15; 3:7) adds to the drama of the prophet's message as well as the repeated use of vocatives: "O inhabitants" (1:11), "O nation" (2:1), "O Canaan" (2:5), and "O Cushites" (2:12). The poet's metaphors and similes help to create vivid impressions in the imaginations of the hearers and readers of Zephaniah (see, e.g., 1:17; 2:9, 13; 3:14).

With respect to the book's structure, the poetry of Zephaniah can be divided into the following units:

   I. Superscription (1:1)
  II. Proclamations of judgment and imminent disasters (1:2–3:8)
     Against Jerusalem and Judah (1:2–2:3)
     Against Philistia (2:4-7)
     Against Moab and Ammon (2:8-11)
     Against Ethiopia (2:12)
     Against Assyria (2:13-15)
  III. Statement of reproach against Jerusalem (3:1-7)
  IV. Statement of future purification (3:8-13)
   V. Proclamation of hope, salvation, and restoration (3:14-20)

Icon of Zephaniah, 17th century, North Russia.

Unlike many other prophetic books, Zephaniah features only one main speaker—God, whose speeches reveal a deity full of wrath and hostility toward not only the world's people but also other nonhuman creatures of the earth (1:2-3). This God is completely disgusted with Judah and Jerusalem because of their false and sensual worship (1:4-6; 3:1-5) and is enraged with the nations because of their unjust treatment of Judah (2:8) and their corrupt deeds (3:7). Without a doubt, the book of Zephaniah is a book sure to set one's teeth on edge but, like so many of the Bible's other prophetic books, Zephaniah is not without a word of hope (3:11-20). All of the rage and fury eventually dissipate as daughter Zion looks forward to salvation and restoration in the sight of all peoples.

The theological dimensions of the book of Zephaniah

The most significant theological aspect of the book of Zephaniah is how the prophet portrays Israel's God. Throughout the text, the prophet heralds a fire-and-brimstone God whose quest is for sovereignty over peoples and other gods and whose sense of ethics will not allow for injustice and the inordinate assertion of power of one people over another. In a fit of rage, this God makes no discrimination between the guilty human beings and the nonhumans: all creation will experience the devastating effects of the divine wrath. This divine wrath and anger is understandable, given the state of affairs of Judah, Jerusalem, and the nations in general. What becomes difficult from a hermeneutical viewpoint, however, is the form that the wrath and anger takes: God's actions are destructive and not constructive, punitive and not life-sustaining. These images of an anthropomorphic, androcentric God reflect both the culture of the day and the biblical writer's theological agenda, which is to establish Israel's God not only as sovereign over all nations, peoples, and gods but also as one who is more powerful than the most powerful of nations and peoples on the face of the earth. Israel's God is Lord of creation and Lord of history. Finally, the text makes clear that the divine intent is not for complete annihilation. A remnant will be spared, the nations will be brought into line, and Zion will be restored, but only after all has been divinely chastened and purified, and love is renewed.

Zephaniah

1 ¹The word of the LORD which came to Zephaniah, the son of Cushi, the son of Gedaliah, the son of Amariah, the son of Hezekiah, in the days of Josiah, the son of Amon, king of Judah.

The Day of the Lord: Judgment on Judah

²I will completely sweep away all things
 from the face of the land—oracle of the LORD.
³I will sweep away human being and beast alike,

I will sweep away the birds of the sky,
 and the fish of the sea.
I will make the wicked stumble;
 I will eliminate the people
 from the face of the land—oracle of the LORD.
⁴I will stretch out my hand against Judah,
 and against all the inhabitants of Jerusalem;
I will eliminate from this place
 the last vestige of Baal,
 the name of the idolatrous priests.

SUPERSCRIPTION

Zephaniah 1:1

The book of Zephaniah opens with a simple introductory statement that designates the contents of the book as a word from God, identifies who the prophet Zephaniah is by way of his ancestors, and provides a historical framework for Zephaniah's preaching. The fact that the word of the Lord "came" to Zephaniah makes clear that the prophetic word is a gift, usually flowing from an intuitive kind of religious experience, and not something that can be learned or sought after. Zephaniah's name could mean "YHWH hides" or "YHWH treasures." Zephaniah is the name of a Canaanite god, and thus the name could also mean "Zaphon is YHWH." Zephaniah's father is Cushi, his grandfather is Gedaliah, his great-grandfather is Amariah, and his great-great-grandfather is Hezekiah. Very little is known about any of these men except for Hezekiah, whose name means "the Lord is my strength." Hezekiah was the thirteenth king of Judah and was the son of Ahaz and Abi (2 Kgs 18:2). He conducted a reformation that reached beyond

⁵And those who bow down on the
 roofs
 to the host of heaven,
And those who bow down to the
 LORD
 but swear by Milcom;
⁶And those who have turned away
 from the LORD,
 and those who have not sought
 the LORD,
 who have not inquired of him.

⁷Silence in the presence of the Lord
 GOD!
 for near is the day of the LORD,
Yes, the LORD has prepared a
 sacrifice,
 he has consecrated his guests.
⁸On the day of the LORD's
 sacrifice
I will punish the officials and the
 king's sons,

and all who dress in foreign
 apparel.
⁹I will punish, on that day,
 all who leap over the threshold,
Who fill the house of their master
 with violence and deceit.
¹⁰On that day—oracle of the
 LORD—
A cry will be heard from the Fish
 Gate,
 a wail from the Second Quarter,
 loud crashing from the hills.
¹¹Wail, O inhabitants of Maktesh!
 for all the merchants are
 destroyed,
 all who weigh out silver, done
 away with.

¹²At that time,
I will search Jerusalem with lamps,
 I will punish the people
 who settle like dregs in wine,

Jerusalem to include the cleansing of the land and the tribes of Benjamin, Ephraim, and Manasseh. Hezekiah had a fairly good relationship with the prophet Isaiah. The king had to deal with the aggressive Assyrians and their king, Sennacherib, who was eventually defeated by an angel of the Lord (2 Kgs 19:35). Hezekiah's achievements are recorded in 2 Chronicles 32:27-30. Thus, four generations are represented in the superscription. Zephaniah's roots, then, are in Judah. The prophet is said to have begun his ministry during the reign of Josiah, the sixteenth king of Judah who was the son of Amon and the grandson of Manasseh (2 Kgs 21:23–23:30). Josiah's thirty-one-year reign was characterized by peace, prosperity, and reform. A godly man, he was seriously injured in a battle with the Egyptian pharaoh Necho II and died shortly thereafter. Finally, this superscription is similar to that of Hosea, Joel, Micah, Haggai, and Zechariah, all of which identify the prophetic proclamations as "the word of the LORD."

PROCLAMATIONS OF JUDGMENT AND IMMINENT DISASTERS
Zephaniah 1:2–3:8

The Day of the Lord that Habakkuk was quietly awaiting was drawing near. This day was to be most fierce and terrible, a day of total destruction

Who say in their hearts,
    "The Lord will not do good,
    nor will he do harm."
¹³Their wealth shall be given to
    plunder
    and their houses to devastation;
They will build houses,
    but not dwell in them;
They will plant vineyards,
    but not drink their wine.
¹⁴Near is the great day of the LORD,
    near and very swiftly coming.
The sound of the day of the LORD!
    Piercing—
    there a warrior shrieks!
¹⁵A day of wrath is that day,
    a day of distress and anguish,
    a day of ruin and desolation,

A day of darkness and gloom,
    a day of thick black clouds,
¹⁶A day of trumpet blasts and battle
    cries
    against fortified cities,
    against lofty battlements.
¹⁷I will hem the people in
    till they walk like the blind,
    because they have sinned
    against the LORD;
And their blood shall be poured out
    like dust,
    and their bowels like dung.
¹⁸Neither their silver nor their gold
    will be able to save them.
On the day of the LORD's wrath,
    in the fire of his passion,
    all the earth will be consumed.

---

for Judah, inclusive of human and nonhuman life. Similarly Zephaniah describes a God who is coming with power to deal with the country and Jerusalem's idolatrous and unjust people. In particular, Zephaniah takes issue with Judah's leadership. Some of Judah's officials as well as the king's sons had adopted foreign customs and attire, others engaged in foreign religious practices, and still others were perpetrators of violence and deceit. The historical backdrop to Zephaniah's preaching is the invasion of the Babylonians, whom God is raising up as Judah's enemy to chastise Judah for its transgressions. This section consists of five judgment proclamations that outline imminent disasters for not only Jerusalem and Judah but also for other nations. In these texts one sees an ethnocentric view of God who comes with power to defend Judah by overpowering those countries that have taunted and conquered God's "people." Power is used to overpower, and violence gives birth to more violence.

1:2–2:3 Against Jerusalem and Judah

This first judgment proclamation directed toward Jerusalem and Judah is grand in scope. In verses 2-6 Zephaniah describes the extensive destruction of life that will befall Judah, especially those who have disregarded God and God's ways (1:6). The use of power will be indiscriminate on God's part, and the judgment will be more inclusive than the primeval flood. The reason for such divine wrath is clear from verses 4-6: idolatry, a transgression against the first commandment (Exod 20:2-6). Breach of covenant relationship on the part of human beings reaps repercussions that devastate not only humanity

> For he will make an end, yes, a
> > sudden end,
> of all who live on the earth.
> 2 ¹Gather, gather yourselves together,
> > O nation without shame!
> ²Before you are driven away,
> > like chaff that disappears;
> Before there comes upon you
> > the blazing anger of the LORD;
>
> Before there comes upon you
> > the day of the LORD's anger.
> ³Seek the LORD,
> > all you humble of the land,
> > who have observed his law;
> Seek justice,
> > seek humility;
> Perhaps you will be sheltered
> > on the day of the LORD's anger.

but also the natural world. The reference to Baal in verse 4 is the storm god, the son of El, who is the chief Canaanite god. Baal was the god of rain and the giver of fertility. He was sometimes referred to as the husband of the land. Originally the word meant "lord" or "owner" (e.g., Exod 21:28-29) or "husband" (e.g., Exod 21:3). By the time of the Late Bronze Age, Baal then became a title for various gods and also the name of El's son. Worship of Baal took place on hills or mountaintops (1 Kgs 12:31; 2 Kgs 17:9-10; 23:8, 13, 15).

Verse 7 contains an admonition to be silent before God, who is close at hand, and is followed by a description of the transgressions of which some members of Judah are guilty. In this verse the prophet also announces what God intends to do to those guilty of transgression. The officials and the king's sons who wear foreign attire are most likely guilty of Baal worship (2 Kgs 10:22) and therefore apostasy. Those who leap over the threshold (1:9) are guilty of a superstition that holds that evil spirits lurk at a doorway, waiting to enter if one steps on the threshold, an act that would let the spirits in. Because these two acts are associated with apostasy, those who engage in them will experience divine punishment. The wealthy who smugly believe that God is indifferent (1:12) will also experience God's punishment: their wealth will be plundered, and their houses and vineyards will come to naught (1:13). The Day of the Lord (1:7, 14) will be a day of divine wrath, sadness, wailing, and economic distress (1:2-13).

In 1:14-16 the description of the Day of the Lord continues. Hastening ever closer, this day will be full of wrath, distress, anguish, ruin, devastation, darkness, gloom, and clouds, with the sound of battle directed against Judah.

The description begun in 1:8-9 of what God plans to do to some people continues in 1:17-18: the inhabitants of the land will lose a sense of direction for their lives and will be slaughtered (1:17). Money will not buy them any security because the whole earth will be consumed (1:18).

This Day of the Lord is hyperbolic and symbolizes God's extraordinary rage over the central sin of some of the people: apostasy. God will not tolerate Judah worshiping other gods. The warfare language emerges from the social

Judgment on the Nations

⁴For Gaza shall be forsaken,
and Ashkelon shall be a waste,
Ashdod they shall drive out at
midday,
and Ekron shall be uprooted.
⁵Ah! You who dwell by the
seacoast,
the nation of Cherethites,
the word of the LORD is against
you!
O Canaan, land of the Philistines,
I will leave you to perish without an inhabitant!

⁶You shall become fields for
shepherds,
and folds for flocks.
⁷The seacoast shall belong
to the remnant of the house of
Judah;
by the sea they shall pasture.
In the houses of Ashkelon
they shall lie down in the
evening.
For the LORD their God will take
care of them,
and bring about their
restoration.

location of the Judahites. Finally, the text as a whole portrays God as a violent and somewhat unjust God who threatens to sweep away everything because some people have sinned.

The last section of the poem is an exhortation. The prophet calls Judah to make restitution and to turn back to God before the Day of the Lord and the threatened divine wrath become a reality (2:1-3ab). If the people turn aside from their ways and seek right relationship once more, then perhaps they "will be sheltered on the day of the LORD's anger" (2:3c). The mission of the prophet, then, is not only to expose transgression but also to hold out hope to a struggling people.

2:4-7 Against Philistia

The Day of the Lord will affect not only Jerusalem and Judah but many other nations as well. The first nation to be affected is Philistia (cf. Ezek 25:15-17). Gaza, Ashkelon, Ashdod, and Ekron (2:4) are all cities of the Phi-listine confederation. The Cherethites (2:5) are a synonym for, or a subdivi-sion of, the Philistines. The Cherethites may be associated with Crete, which is part of the larger Aegean region from where the Philistines came. The Philistine coastal plain will be void of human inhabitants and, thus, the area will become a pastureland where shepherds can pasture their flocks (2:6). The shepherds are Judeans. Interestingly, even though the image in 2:4-5 is one of devastation, the land itself will continue on as a sign of life with life-sustaining possibilities. In 2:7 the plot thickens: the Judeans will not only pasture their flocks on land that once belonged to the Philistines but they will also pasture them by the seacoast, which will become the lot of the Judahites as well (2:7). Thus, embedded in this judgment proclamation against Philistia is a word of hope for Judah (2:6-7).

⁸I have heard the taunts uttered by
Moab,
and the insults of the Ammonites,
When they taunted my people
and made boasts against their
territory.
⁹Therefore, as I live—
oracle of the LORD of hosts—
the God of Israel,
Moab shall become like Sodom,
the Ammonites like Gomorrah:
A field of weeds,
a salt pit,
a waste forever.
The remnant of my people shall
plunder them,
the survivors of my nation
dispossess them.
¹⁰This will be the recompense for
their pride,

because they taunted and
boasted against
the people of the LORD of hosts.
¹¹The LORD shall inspire them with
terror
when he makes all the gods of
earth waste away;
Then the distant shores of the
nations,
each from its own place,
shall bow down to him.

¹²You too, O Cushites,
shall be slain by the sword of
the LORD.
¹³He will stretch out his hand
against the north,
to destroy Assyria;
He will make Nineveh a waste,
dry as the desert.

2:8-11 Against Moab and Ammon

In this third judgment speech the target of God's wrath is Moab and
Ammon (cf. Gen 19:30-38; Isa 15; Jer 48–49:6; Ezek 25:1-11). These two nations were Judah's neighbors to the east across the Jordan River. Both the
Moabites and the Ammonites have poked fun at the Judahites—God's
"people"—and have gloated over their territory (2:8). Therefore Israel's God
will deal terribly with these two groups; and ironically, the plunderers will
be the ones despoiled by those whom they have attacked (2:9-10). For reference to Sodom and Gomorrah, see Genesis 19:1-29. Israel's God as the
sovereign one over all other gods and the conversion of the nations to
worshiping God is the focus of 2:11.

2:12 Against Ethiopia

The fourth judgment speech is directed toward Ethiopia (cf. Isa 18:1-6),
also known as Cush, whose inhabitants are Cushites who will be slain by
the Lord's sword, a dreadful weapon, sharpened, polished, flashing, and
always ready for slaughter (cf. Ezek 21:1-17).

2:13-15 Against Assyria

What Nahum foresaw, Zephaniah sees as well—the destruction of
Nineveh and the Assyrians. This fifth judgment speech is addressed to Assyria and its capital city Nineveh. Animal imagery reinforces the city's total

¹⁴In her midst flocks shall lie down,
all the wild life of the hollows;
The screech owl and the desert owl
shall roost in her columns;
The owl shall hoot from the
window,
the raven croak from the
doorway.
¹⁵Is this the exultant city
that dwelt secure,
That told itself,
"I and there is no one else"?
How it has become a waste,
a lair for wild animals!
Those who pass by it
hiss, and shake their fists!

Jerusalem Reproached

3 ¹Ah! Rebellious and polluted,
the tyrannical city!
²It listens to no voice,
accepts no correction;
In the LORD it has not trusted,
nor drawn near to its God.
³Its officials within it
are roaring lions;
Its judges are desert wolves

that have no bones to gnaw by
morning.
⁴Its prophets are reckless,
treacherous people;
Its priests profane what is holy,
and do violence to the law.
⁵But the LORD in its midst is just,
doing no wrong;
Morning after morning rendering
judgment
unfailingly, at dawn;
the wicked, however, know no
shame.

⁶I have cut down nations,
their battlements are laid waste;
I have made their streets deserted,
with no one passing through;
Their cities are devastated,
with no one dwelling in them.
⁷I said, "Surely now you will fear
me,
you will accept correction;
They cannot fail to see
all I have brought upon them."
Yet the more eagerly they have done
all their corrupt deeds.

destruction. Once a secure and exultant city, Nineveh will become a wilderness for animals.

STATEMENT OF REPROACH AGAINST JERUSALEM

Zephaniah 3:1-7

In Zephaniah 3:1-7, focus shifts from judgment speeches against foreign countries to a statement of reproach against Jerusalem. Verses 1-5 portray God taking Jerusalem to task for a variety of reasons: it is obdurate, belligerent, and distant from God (3:2). Animal imagery metaphorically describes the city's political leadership: officials and judges are ferocious and fierce; they prey on those under their authority (3:3). Its religious leaders are just as bad: the prophets are reckless, treacherous persons; its priests have profaned the sacred and have done violence to the law (3:4). The one who stands in sharp contrast to all of those persons is God, who acts justly every day (3:5). Verse 5 contrasts the unjust with God, imaged metaphorically as a judge.

The Nations Punished and Jerusalem Restored

⁸Therefore, wait for me—oracle of
the Lord—
until the day when I arise as
accuser;
For it is my decision to gather
nations,
to assemble kingdoms,
In order to pour out upon them my
wrath,
all my blazing anger;
For in the fire of my passion
all the earth will be consumed.

⁹For then I will make pure
the speech of the peoples,
That they all may call upon the
name of the Lord,
to serve him with one accord;
¹⁰From beyond the rivers of
Ethiopia
and as far as the recesses of the
North,
they shall bring me offerings.

¹¹On that day
You will not be ashamed
of all your deeds,
when you rebelled against me;
For then I will remove from your
midst
the proud braggarts,
And you shall no longer exalt yourself
on my holy mountain.
¹²But I will leave as a remnant in
your midst
a people humble and lowly,
Who shall take refuge in the name
of the Lord—
¹³the remnant of Israel.
They shall do no wrong
and speak no lies;
Nor shall there be found in their
mouths
a deceitful tongue;
They shall pasture and lie down
with none to disturb them.

Verse 6 recalls the types of judgments God has meted out in the past.
God has cut off countries, turned battlements into ruins, laid waste streets,
and made cities desolate. Historically all of these events reflect the Assyrian
devastation of Judah during Hezekiah's reign. The invasion was attributed
to God on account of the people's wickedness.

God now hopes that in its present state, Jerusalem will recall this past
experience, take note of what happens when one acts wickedly, accept correction, and not lose sight of all that God has brought upon it (3:6-7). God
hopes Jerusalem will learn from the past and fall in line with God's authority
and leadership, lest it too will have to suffer more punitive consequences.
God, however, observes that Jerusalem's inhabitants have done their corrupt
deeds more eagerly (3:7).

STATEMENT OF FUTURE PURIFICATION

Zephaniah 3:8-13

Following the five judgment speeches and a reproach against Jerusalem,
Jerusalem is now called upon to wait for the Lord, who will surely pour out

◄ ⁱ⁴Shout for joy, daughter Zion!
  sing joyfully, Israel!
Be glad and exult with all your
  heart,
  daughter Jerusalem!ʰ
ⁱ⁵The LORD has removed the
  judgment
  against you,
  he has turned away your
    enemies;
The King of Israel, the LORD, is in
  your midst,
  you have no further misfortune
    to fear.
ⁱ⁶On that day, it shall be said to
  Jerusalem:
Do not fear, Zion,
  do not be discouraged!

ⁱ⁷The LORD, your God, is in your ▶
  midst,
  a mighty savior,
Who will rejoice over you with
  gladness,
  and renew you in his love,
Who will sing joyfully because of
  you,
ⁱ⁸as on festival days.

I will remove disaster from among
  you,
  so that no one may recount your
    disgrace.
ⁱ⁹At that time I will deal
  with all who oppress you;
I will save the lame,
  and assemble the outcasts;

---

divine wrath upon the nations (3:8). The reference to God arising as an accuser hints at a lawsuit that God has against his people. Verse 9 indicates the type of purification that is to occur: the foreign countries will be given pure lips so that they can all worship Israel's God and bring gifts to this God as well (3:10). In verse 11 God, speaking through the prophet, directs attention to Judah. Prior to judgment, the wicked political and religious leaders in Jerusalem were too bold to feel any shame for their behavior even though such behavior turned Jerusalem into a rebellious, polluted, and oppressive city (3:1-5). After God's purifying judgment, the city and its inhabitants will no longer have to feel shame on account of their behavior because their perpetrators will be gone (3:11). The population that will remain in Jerusalem—the remnant—will be a "humble and lowly" people (3:12), a people of integrity who have obeyed God and have sought righteousness (2:3). Their security will be in their God, and they will enjoy abiding peace (3:13).

PROCLAMATION OF HOPE, SALVATION, AND RESTORATION

Zephaniah 3:14-20

Words of judgment, reproach, and purification lead to words of hope, salvation, and restoration. Addressed to daughter Zion—daughter Jerusalem—now chastened and purified, Zephaniah calls upon the city to shout with joy and sing joyfully (3:14). Why? Because God had removed the judgment against the city, has turned away all the enemies (cf. 1:2–3:8, 15), and

I will give them praise and renown in every land where they were shamed. ²⁰At that time I will bring you home, and at that time I will gather you;	For I will give you renown and praise, among all the peoples of the earth, When I bring about your restoration before your very eyes, says the LORD.

I will give them praise and renown
   in every land where they were
     shamed.
²⁰At that time I will bring you
   home,
and at that time I will gather
   you;

---

now dwells in their midst (3:15). The phrase "On that day" (3:16) is eschatological and points to a future new day for Jerusalem. No longer will Jerusalem and its inhabitants experience the "Day of the Lord," a day of wrath (1:2–2:3). The phrase "Do not fear, Zion" (3:16) is a typical reassurance formula (cf. Gen 15:1; 21:17; 35:17; Exod 20:20; Isa 7:4; 35:4; 40:9; 41:10; Jer 30:10; Joel 2:21; Hag 2:5; Ruth 3:11). These verses foreshadow the end of the Babylonian exile and the return of the Judahites to their land. Because God dwells in Jerusalem and in its inhabitants' midst (3:17), there is a reason to celebrate. Jerusalem's disgrace will no longer be remembered by others because God is about to remove disaster from the city's midst (3:17d). A city and a people now purified will soon be made glorious through God's transformative love (3:18). Jerusalem is reassured that God will deal with the city's oppressors (3:19a). Verses 19b-20 present a joyous picture. With right relationship renewed, God will gather the peoples together, bring them home, restore them, and make them glorious throughout the earth (3:20). Finally, like all of the prophets in this commentary, Zephaniah's final proclamation is a word of hope, which is at the heart of the prophetic vocation and mission.

Habakkuk

Written with brevity and candor, the book of Habakkuk delivers chilling words of judgment upon the people of Judah prior to the destruction and collapse of the holy city Jerusalem, the temple, and the southern kingdom Judah. One of the striking features of the book of Habakkuk is its dialogical style. God and the prophet Habakkuk have an honest, oftentimes heartrending, conversation about life and events in the seventh century B.C. On more than one occasion, Habakkuk complains to God, challenging God about a lack of divine responsiveness to the destruction and violence that surrounds the prophet upon which he must look day after day (1:1-4). Habakkuk's complaints do not go unanswered; God does respond and assures the prophet that, indeed, justice will be served. The book closes on a poignant note: the prophet prays to his God and in his prayer, he acknowledges God's wondrous power. Habakkuk places all his trust in this God who is the prophet's strength and who makes his feet like the feet of deer, swift and agile to "tread upon the heights" (3:19).

The world of Habakkuk

The book of Habakkuk reflects the times of the seventh century B.C. The southern kingdom Judah and its inhabitants stand on the brink of ruin and exile; the fall of Jerusalem and the destruction of the temple are imminently on the horizon. At this time, Babylon is Judah's greatest threat, and ironically, God is said to be rousing up the Babylonians against the Judahites (1:6). Through the brute force of the Babylonians, Israel's God will chastise the inhabitants of Judah because of their injustices, which include greed, theft, embezzlement, extortion, debauchery, and idolatry. Important to note is that the biblical text makes reference to the "Chaldeans," a name used interchangeably and synonymous with the name "Babylonians" (see, e.g., Isa 47:1; Jer 25:12).

During the seventh century B.C. and after the Babylonians' victory over the Egyptians at Carchemish in 605 B.C., the Judahites began paying tribute to the Babylonians. The tide began to turn, however, when Judah's king

Jehoiakim rebelled against Babylonian control. As a result of such rebellion, the Babylonians attacked Jerusalem in 597 b.c. and deported both the royal family as well as prominent citizens living in Judah. Succeeding Jehoiakim was Zedekiah, who supported Babylonian control at the beginning of his reign but who later revolted against such control. The revolt triggered the return of the Babylonian armies, who marched into Jerusalem and destroyed it in 587 b.c. This action marked the end of the southern kingdom Judah. The message of Habakkuk is directed to Judah during the time of crisis that led up to Judah's demise by the Babylonians. The actual dating of the book, however, remains a topic of debate.

With respect to the prophet Habakkuk, very little is known about his background, and, like the other prophets of ancient biblical times, whether or not he was an actual historical person is a topic of lively debate. Another topic of discussion is the question of Habakkuk's vocation. Habakkuk may have been a cultic prophet stationed in the temple, or a visionary, or even just an ordinary individual concerned about the events and issues of his day. The general consensus is that Habakkuk was a cultic prophet. Whether or not Habakkuk was an actual person, a cultic prophet, a visionary, or an ordinary human being is second to his profound and prophetic message. Habakkuk is deeply concerned about the injustices he sees within his community, and he is unhappy with the various prophetic theologies of history that resolve the injustices through the use of foreign powers as God's way of chastising Judah.

The literary dimensions of the book of Habakkuk

The text of Habakkuk moves at a lively pace primarily because of the dynamic dialogue that occurs between God and Habakkuk. The addresses and exchanges that take place come to life through the repetitive use of literary techniques such as direct address (1:2; 3:2), which is also achieved by the use of the pronoun "you" (see, e.g., 1:12, 14; 2:10, 16; 3:9, 13), rhetorical questions (see, e.g., 1:3, 12, 17; 2:13, 18, 19; 3:8), the use of imperative verb forms (see, e.g., 1:5; 2:2b, 4), and the cataloging of a series of woe prophecies (2:6b-8, 9-11, 12-14, 15-17, 18-19). Metaphorical language depicts a multifaceted picture of God as "holy God" (1:12), "Rock" (1:12), one who not only listens but also responds (1:2–2:1; 2:2-20), radiant (3:3-4), powerful (3:5-7), and an enraged warrior who will act on behalf of justice (3:2-15). According to the prophet Habakkuk, however, divine justice may not be done in the same direct way as may have been perceived at other junctures of Israel and Judah's history. In the book of Habakkuk, God is seen not so much as a warrior but more like a "commander-in-chief" who will send the Chaldeans (1:6) to deal with the inhabitants and the land of Judah.

The prophet Habakkuk, sculpted by Aleijadinho, in front of the church of the Sanctuary of Bom Jesus of Matosinhos at Congonhas, Minas Gerais, Brazil.

With respect to the text's structure, the book of Habakkuk can be divided into the following units and subunits:

   I. Superscription (1:1)
  II. The prophet's first complaint (1:2-4)
 III. A divine response (1:5-11)
 IV. The prophet's second complaint (1:12–2:1)
  V. A divine response: a vision statement with five woes (2:2-20)
 VI. A prophet's prayer (3:1-19)

The theological dimensions of the book of Habakkuk

From the text of Habakkuk, four theological themes emerge: (1) a concern for rampant injustice, (2) an effort at presenting God as powerful and just in the face of injustice, (3) an assertion that righteousness and faith are inseparable, and (4) God as one's hope and salvation in times of trouble. The text's portrayal of God is in need of ongoing critical theological reflection and discussion. For example, the text depicts God in 1:5-11 as one who raises up the Chaldeans, "that bitter and impulsive people," for the purpose of meting out divine punitive justice to Judah because of the land's apostate and lawless ways (see, e.g., 1:2-17). This God has the potential of reducing people to fish and "creeping things" (1:14), as the "wicked devour those more just than themselves" (1:13). Yet this is the same God who empowers the prophet Habakkuk by giving him a vision. This vision is dreadful for the Judahites who oppress others but hopeful for the victims of injustice (see, e.g., 2:2-19). The text also offers a mixed view of divine power. In Habakkuk 3:2-15, the prophet's prayer provides a clear yet metaphorical portrait of God's power in relation to the whole of creation, for instance, how God "shook the earth" and "made the nations tremble" (3:6), how God "came forth" with power to "save [the] anointed one" (3:13), and so forth. According to Habakkuk 3, God has power over heaven, earth, kingdoms, the natural world, and people. All of these elements pale before or on account of such power, with the exception of the prophet, for whom God is his salvation and strength (3:18-19). Thus, the book of Habakkuk presents divine power as a force that has devastating effects. Finally, the book of Habakkuk is a glorious portrait of one person's faith in his God. This faith dares to question and challenge God's actions and motives, and this faith is bold enough and brave enough to let go to God in trust, who will, in the end, save the needy from the hands of evildoers (3:13, 18-19).

Habakkuk

1 ¹The oracle which Habakkuk the prophet received in a vision.

Habakkuk's First Complaint

²How long, O LORD, must I cry for help
and you do not listen?
Or cry out to you, "Violence!"
and you do not intervene?

³Why do you let me see iniquity?
why do you simply gaze at evil?
Destruction and violence are before me;
there is strife and discord.
⁴This is why the law is numb
and justice never comes,
For the wicked surround the just;
this is why justice comes forth perverted.

SUPERSCRIPTION

Habakkuk 1:1

The opening words of the book of Habakkuk introduce and define Habakkuk as a prophet and make clear that what is about to be proclaimed is the contents of a vision (cf. Isa 1:1; Obad 1:1; Nah 1:1). The message is a divine gift.

THE PROPHET'S FIRST COMPLAINT

Habakkuk 1:2-4

With a series of heartrending questions, Habakkuk begins the dialogue with God. In the first two rhetorical questions, Habakkuk asks God why he, the prophet, is not being answered when he cries out for help (cf. Exod 3:7), and why God is not saving him when he shouts out, "Violence!" (cf. Jer 20:7). One can appreciate the prophet's perplexity, especially since he knows from his religious tradition that God has rescued the innocent from the hands of the wicked in the past. Habakkuk poses two more rhetorical questions in verse 3 and asks why he must see iniquity. He also indirectly challenges God by asking why the Holy One of Israel just gazes on evil. Implied is that God sees all the wrongdoing and trouble but does nothing to change the situation

God's Response

⁵Look over the nations and see!
  Be utterly amazed!
For a work is being done in your
    days
  that you would not believe,
      were it told.
⁶For now I am raising up the
    Chaldeans,
  that bitter and impulsive people,
Who march the breadth of the land
  to take dwellings not their own.
⁷They are terrifying and dreadful;
  their right and their exalted
      position are of their own
      making.
⁸Swifter than leopards are their
    horses,
and faster than desert wolves.
Their horses spring forward;
  they come from far away;
  they fly like an eagle hastening
      to devour.
⁹All of them come for violence,
  their combined onslaught, a
      stormwind
  to gather up captives like sand.
¹⁰They scoff at kings,
  ridicule princes;
They laugh at any fortress,
  heap up an earthen ramp, and
      conquer it.
¹¹Then they sweep through like the
    wind and vanish—
  they make their own strength
      their god!

---

of destruction, violence, strife, and discord. In verse 4, he contends that the law is basically useless because it is either misapplied and distorted or not enforced at all. Furthermore, God's failure to act against the wicked renders the Deuteronomic law ineffective with respect to enforcing justice. The identity of the wicked seems to be oppressors within the Judahite community itself. Thus, verses 2-4 are an individual lament that takes the form of a complaint. The phrase "how long" is typical of complaints (cf. Exod 16:28; Num 14:11; Ps 13:1; 62:3; Job 18:2; 19:2).

A DIVINE RESPONSE

Habakkuk 1:5-11

Habakkuk's complaint does not go unheard. Verses 5-11 are God's response to the prophet's lament. Habakkuk learns that God will act on behalf of the suffering righteous by raising up a "bitter and impulsive people"—the Chaldeans—to defeat Judah's wicked (1:5-6). Chaldeans is another term for Babylonians. Verses 6-11 describe the Chaldeans/Babylonians vividly. They are fierce, impetuous, and without a sense of justice. They use their power to oppress others (1:6) and they make up their own rules (1:7). The annual images associated with them denote both speed and ferociousness: they all "come for violence" (1:8-9). No one and nothing will render them powerless (1:10). Their own might is their god (1:11). In response to his complaint, Habakkuk has received a word of judgment that he must now deliver to his

Habakkuk's Second Complaint

¹²Are you not from of old, O LORD,
my holy God, immortal?
LORD, you have appointed them for
judgment,
O Rock, you have set them in
place to punish!
¹³Your eyes are too pure to look
upon wickedness,
and the sight of evil you cannot
endure.
Why, then, do you gaze on the
faithless in silence
while the wicked devour those
more just than
themselves?
¹⁴You have made mortals like the
fish in the sea,
like creeping things without a
leader.
¹⁵He brings them all up with a
hook,
and hauls them away with his
net;
He gathers them in his fishing net,
and then rejoices and exults.
¹⁶Therefore he makes sacrifices to
his net,
and burns incense to his fishing
net;
For thanks to them his portion is
rich,
and his meal lavish.
¹⁷Shall they, then, keep on drawing
his sword
to slaughter nations without
mercy?

2 ¹I will stand at my guard post,
and station myself upon the
rampart;
I will keep watch to see what he
will say to me,
and what answer he will give to
my complaint.

---

people. The passage begs the question: What kind of a God would use an empire, especially a violent and unjust one, to deal with another kingdom's injustices? Historically, Habakkuk's prophecy foreshadows the Babylonian invasion of Judah and its demise, an inevitable event and one that the poet attributes to God in hopes that the wicked in Judah will change their ways. They do not, and the Babylonians do invade Judah in 598 B.C.

THE PROPHET'S SECOND COMPLAINT

Habakkuk 1:12–2:1

Habakkuk is shocked by God's response and in verses 12-14 he once again uses rhetorical questions to reprove God for God's silence and inaction. While God has designated the Babylonians to act against Judah's wicked ones, Habakkuk's question suggests his discomfort with God's plan (1:13). Are not the people of Judah more righteous than their Babylonian enemies? Yet God is silent, allowing the Babylonians to overtake the people of Judah. Habakkuk suggests that they are like fish and crawling things that have no ruler to deliver them (1:14). God's "silence" seems to give more power to the wicked ones. The reference to God as "immortal" in verse 12 may be an allusion to the dying god of the Mot-Baal myth. Israel's God is

God's Response

²Then the LORD answered me and
said:
Write down the vision;
Make it plain upon tablets,
so that the one who reads it may
run.
³For the vision is a witness for the
appointed time,
a testimony to the end; it will
not disappoint.
If it delays, wait for it,
it will surely come, it will not be
late.
⁴See, the rash have no integrity;
but the just one who is righteous
because of faith shall live.

Sayings Against Tyrants

⁵Indeed wealth is treacherous;
a proud man does not succeed.
He who opens wide his throat like
Sheol,
and is insatiable as death,
Who gathers to himself all the
nations,
and collects for himself all the
peoples—
⁶Shall not all these take up a taunt
against him,
and make a riddle about him,
saying:
Ah! you who store up what is not
yours
—how long can it last!—

---

not supposed to be like Mot-Baal. Israel's God is to be a God of decisive action. The term "Rock," also in verse 12, is a common reference for God (Gen 49:24; Deut 32:4, 15, 18, 30, 31; 2 Sam 22:2; 23:3; Ps 89:26; Isa 30:29, etc.). Clearly, the prophet is disgusted with God's noninvolvement and challenges God's aloofness.

In verses 15-17, Habakkuk metaphorically describes how the king of Babylon treats people—he is like a fisherman who keeps dragging his net again and again to catch more and more fish so that he can increase his own lot. The "net" is an ancient Mesopotamian symbol associated with military power. In the cosmogonic myth, Marduk uses a net to conquer Tiamet. The fisherman attending his net and seine in verse 16 symbolizes the Babylonians' trust in their military power that brought them great wealth at others' expense. Habakkuk persists in questioning God (1:17) to address the fact that God is allowing the Babylonians to kill nation after nation, ruthlessly. How can God allow such things to happen, and are these slaughters truly the way to establishing justice? Habakkuk 2:1 closes the prophet's complaint; Habakkuk remains vigilant.

A DIVINE RESPONSE: A VISION STATEMENT WITH FIVE WOES

Habakkuk 2:2-20

In verses 2-4, God commands Habakkuk to write down the vision, which will consist of five woes (2:5-20). God assures the prophet that indeed the

you who load yourself down
with collateral.
⁷Will your debtors not rise
suddenly?
Will they not awake, those who
make you tremble?
You will become their spoil!
⁸Because you plundered many
nations,
the remaining peoples shall
plunder you;
Because of the shedding of human
blood,
and violence done to the land,
to the city and to all who live in
it.

⁹Ah! you who pursue evil gain for
your household,
setting your nest on high
to escape the reach of misfortune!
¹⁰You have devised shame for your
household,
cutting off many peoples,
forfeiting your own life;
¹¹For the stone in the wall shall cry
out,
and the beam in the frame shall
answer it!

¹²Ah! you who build a city by
bloodshed,
and who establish a town with
injustice!
¹³Is this not from the LORD of hosts:
peoples toil for what the flames
consume,
and nations grow weary for
nothing!
¹⁴But the earth shall be filled
with the knowledge of the
LORD's glory,
just as the water covers the sea.

¹⁵Ah! you who give your neighbors
the cup of your wrath to drink,
and make them drunk,
until their nakedness is seen!
¹⁶You are filled with shame instead
of glory;
drink, you too, and stagger!
The cup from the LORD's right hand
shall come around to you,
and utter shame shall cover
your glory.
¹⁷For the violence done to Lebanon
shall cover you,
and the destruction of the
animals shall terrify you;

---

vision is a witness for the appointed time that will surely arrive even if at first it is delayed.

Verses 6-20 are a series of woe sayings. To whom they are addressed is not clear. Possibilities include the Babylonians, Judahites, other foreign countries, or the wicked in general. The first four woes present a picture of how some people have used their power to benefit themselves at the expense of others (2:6-17). The first woe is a word of doom for robbers, thieves, embezzlers, and deceitful ones (2:6-8). The second woe is doom for exploiters and extortionists (2:9-11). The third woe condemns evil and violence (2:12-14). The fourth woe casts judgment on debauchery (2:15-17). The fifth woe condemns idolatry and is different from all the others (2:18-20). In verse 16 the cup is a powerful metaphor. No doubt it is the cup of God's wrath (see Obadiah). Iniquity will not be the final word; justice will prevail. The fifth woe is different. People are upbraided for their trust in idols. Undergirding

Because of the shedding of human
blood,
and violence done to the land,
to the city and to all who live in
it.
¹⁸Of what use is the carved image,
that its maker should carve it?
Or the molten image, the lying
oracle,
that its very maker should trust
in it,
and make mute idols?
¹⁹Ah! you who say to wood,
"Awake!"
to silent stone, "Arise!"
Can any such thing give
oracles?
It is only overlaid with gold and
silver,
there is no breath in it at all.
²⁰But the Lord is in his holy temple;
silence before him, all the earth!

Hymn About God's Reign

3 ¹Prayer of Habakkuk, the prophet.
According to Shigyonot.

²O Lord, I have heard your renown,
and am in awe, O Lord, of your
work.

In the course of years revive it,
in the course of years make
yourself known;
in your wrath remember
compassion!

³God came from Teman,
the Holy One from Mount
Paran.

Selah

His glory covered the heavens,
and his praise filled the earth;
⁴his splendor spread like the
light.
He raised his horns high,
he rejoiced on the day of his
strength.
⁵Before him went pestilence,
and plague followed in his
steps.
⁶He stood and shook the earth;
he looked and made the nations
tremble.
Ancient mountains were shattered,
the age-old hills bowed low,
age-old orbits collapsed.

⁷The tents of Cushan trembled,
the pavilions of the land of
Midian.

---

the expression of justice is the law of retaliation, *lex talionis*. Guilty parties
will suffer the same harm they have incurred.

A PROPHET'S PRAYER

Habakkuk 3:1-19

Habakkuk's prayer opens with a simple superscription (3:1). This prayer,
on behalf of the king and his people, is an intercessory one meant to be sung
by the congregation or one representing the congregation. The superscription is followed by a series of statements that acknowledge God's great
deeds and a request that God perform these deeds again but with a spirit
of compassion and not wrath (3:2). Verses 3-15 portray God as a warrior and
celebrate God's power over creation and nations. Embedded in the warrior

⁸Was your anger against the rivers,
    O Lord?
  your wrath against the rivers,
  your rage against the sea,
That you mounted your steeds,
  your victorious chariot?
⁹You readied your bow,
  you filled your bowstring with
    arrows.

          Selah

You split the earth with rivers;
  ¹⁰at the sight of you the
    mountains writhed.
The clouds poured down water;
  the deep roared loudly.
The sun forgot to rise,
  ¹¹the moon left its lofty station,
At the light of your flying arrows,
  at the gleam of your flashing
    spear.

¹²In wrath you marched on the
    earth,
  in fury you trampled the nations.
¹³You came forth to save your
    people,
  to save your anointed one.
You crushed the back of the wicked,
  you laid him bare, bottom to
    neck.

          Selah

¹⁴You pierced his head with your
    shafts;

his princes you scattered with
    your stormwind,
  as food for the poor in unknown
    places.
¹⁵You trampled the sea with your
    horses
  amid the churning of the deep
    waters.

¹⁶I hear, and my body trembles;
  at the sound, my lips quiver.
Decay invades my bones,
  my legs tremble beneath me.
I await the day of distress
  that will come upon the people
    who attack us.

¹⁷For though the fig tree does not
    blossom,
  and no fruit appears on the vine,
Though the yield of the olive fails
  and the terraces produce no
    nourishment,
Though the flocks disappear from
    the fold
  and there is no herd in the stalls,
¹⁸Yet I will rejoice in the Lord
  and exult in my saving God.
¹⁹God, my Lord, is my strength;
  he makes my feet swift as those
    of deer
  and enables me to tread upon
    the heights.

For the leader; with stringed instruments.

God image is the storm god, who often is pictured in Syria-Palestine, standing with a lightning bolt in hand, ready to blaze forth. Waiting for the day of calamity, the prophet becomes queasy and physically uneasy (3:16). The prayer closes on a note of hope (3:17-19). Awaiting justice for those who oppress, the prophet expresses his hope in God, who is the one who saves and the one who strengthens. These verses reflect the richness of Israel's hymnic tradition.

REVIEW AIDS AND DISCUSSION TOPICS

The Book of Amos *(pages 7–36)*

1. What do we know about the historical setting in which Amos lived?

2. What literary techniques does Amos use?

3. Why does Amos choose to portray God as wrathful and overpowering?

4. Amos sometimes depicts God as a warrior and uses warfare imagery. Why does he use these kinds of images (1:3-5)?

5. Why does Amos show God responding to violence with more violence (2:1-3)?

6. Explain the importance of the imagery of fire in Amos 2:5.

7. What groups of people were considered to be the most vulnerable in Israelite society (2:6-16)?

8. How is foreshadowing used in Amos 3:3-15?

9. Describe how agricultural metaphors are used in Amos 4:1-5.

10. What did people in ancient Israel believe resulted from God's blessing and God's curse (4:6-13)?

11. Why was God destructive of the natural world (4:6-10; 8:7-14)?

12. Give a summary of the "three woes" in chapters 5 and 6.

13. Why is God so oppressive in the third woe (6:1-14)?

14. List the five visions in chapters 7–9.

15. What social injustices were present in Israelite society (8:4-14)?

16. What does Amos reveal about power in a hierarchical society (8:4-14)?

17. Describe Amos's change of tone at the end of the book.

The Book of Hosea *(pages 37–74)*

1. What is the historical background of this book?

2. What are the thematic similarities between the books of Amos and Hosea?

3. Hosea uses many metaphors in his book. Describe the challenges that some of these metaphors present when interpreting them in today's society.

4. What metaphor is used to compare to covenant love? What is both positive and negative about the use of this metaphor?

5. What is the significance of the name Jezreel (ch. 1)?

6. Describe the husband-wife metaphor of Hosea/God and Gomer/Israel in chapter 2. What are the contemporary theological challenges of this metaphor?

7. How does Hosea connect humanity with the natural world in the end of chapter 2?

8. Describe how Hosea connects human sinfulness with suffering of the land in 4:1-3.

9. What ethical challenges are raised by the text in Hosea 4:4-19?

10. What is the theological significance of Hosea 6:6?

11. The people of Israel have two faults that prevent them from returning to God. What are they (7:10)?

12. How does Hosea 8:5-6 relate to Exodus 32:1-35?

13. Explain the significance of the "calf of Samaria" (8:6).

14. What similes are used in Hosea 9:10-14 and what are their meanings?

15. How could Hosea 11:1-11 be considered "the window to God's heart," and how does this poem depict God?

16. How should we interpret the violent images of Hosea 13:2–14:1?

17. Describe how the book of Hosea ends on a positive note.

The Book of Micah *(pages 75–103)*

1. Who are considered the four great prophets of the eighth century B.C.?

2. Describe the historical setting of the time period in which this book was written.

3. What are the issues of authenticity of the book of Micah?

4. Discuss the theological themes of this book, especially Micah's depictions of God.

5. What is the biblical significance of the phrase "the heights of the earth" (1:3)?

6. How is God depicted in Micah 1:2-7?

7. Describe how Micah 2:1-5 relates to the *lex talionis.*

8. What does Micah say about Israel's political leaders in 3:1-4?

9. Are the prophets who are denounced in Micah 3:5-7 considered to be "false" prophets?

10. What gifts does Micah claim to have in 3:8?

11. Describe the similarities and differences in the books of Micah and Isaiah regarding a prophetic vision (4:1-5).

12. What does Micah say about war and peace in 4:3-5?

13. Explain how the metaphor of a woman in labor is used in Micah 4:9-10.

14. What are the roles of Zion in Micah 4:10-14?

15. How is idolatry described in Micah 5:11-13?

16. What is the significance of Micah's use of "My people" in 6:3, 5?

17. How should we interpret the subject of human sacrifice in Micah (6:7)?

18. Discuss the importance and relevance of Micah 6:8 in today's world.

19. Describe the similarities between Micah 6:14-15 and passages in Leviticus 26 and Deuteronomy 28.

20. Micah's statements about betrayal of family members was very weighty in Israelite society—why is this (7:6)?

21. How does the prophet Micah interpret the collapse of the northern and southern kingdoms (7:7-10)?

22. The book of Micah also ends optimistically. Describe the portrayal of God here.

The Book of Nahum *(pages 105–14)*

1. What is the historical setting in which this book was written?

2. Describe how Nahum uses war imagery and foreshadowing.

3. What is difficult about this book's imagery from a contemporary view?

4. How does Nahum portray God?

5. Discuss the theological problems raised by how justice is achieved in the book of Nahum.

6. What are the characteristics of God as described in Nahum 1:2-11?

7. What event is celebrated by Judah in Nahum 1:12–2:1?

8. How is metaphorical language used in Nahum 2:6-14?

9. Discuss the principle of *lex talionis* in the book of Nahum (2:2-14).

10. What do the images in Nahum 3:4-5, 13 say about the cultural attitudes toward women at the time?

The Book of Zephaniah *(pages 115–28)*

1. Describe the historical backdrop that the book of Zephaniah reflects.

2. How does Zephaniah use the phrases "on that day" and "I will . . ." in this book?

3. There is only one main speaker in the book of Zephaniah. Who is it?

4. Why does Zephaniah portray God as destructive?

5. What are the possible meanings of the name Zephaniah (1:1)?

6. What is similar about Zephaniah's superscription compared to those of Hosea, Joel, Micah, Haggai, and Zechariah (1:1)?

7. What is the reason for God's wrath in the first judgment proclamation (1:4-6)?

8. Describe the symbolism of the Day of the Lord (1:2–2:3).

9. Why is the Assyrian invasion of Judah attributed to God (3:6)?

10. What does God hope for in Zephaniah 3:6-7?

11. What historical event does Zephaniah 3:14-20 foreshadow?

The Book of Habakkuk *(pages 129–39)*

1. How does the book of Habakkuk reflect the times of the seventh century B.C.?

2. God achieves divine justice a bit differently in this book. How so?

3. In what ways is God portrayed in the book of Habakkuk?

4. What are the challenges that Habakkuk raises to God in 1:2-4?

5. What is God's response to Habakkuk in 1:5-11?

6. What historical event does Habakkuk's prophecy foreshadow (1:5-11)?

7. Why is God referred to as "immortal" in 1:12?

8. Describe the significance of the metaphor of the net (1:15-17).

9. Discuss Habakkuk's fifth woe and its relation to idolatry and *lex talionis* (2:18-20).

10. Habakkuk closes with expressions of hope in God. Discuss the theme of hope with which the Prophetic Books end.

INDEX OF CITATIONS FROM THE
CATECHISM OF THE CATHOLIC CHURCH

The arabic number(s) following the citation refer(s) to the paragraph number(s) in the *Catechism of the Catholic Church*. The asterisk following a paragraph number indicates that the citation has been paraphrased.

Amos		1	762*	11:9	208
5:21-5	2100*	2	218*		
5:24	1435*	2:1	441*	**Micah**	
7:2	2584*	2:7	2380*	2:2	2534*
7:5	2584*	2:21-22	2787*	4:1-4	762*
8:4-10	2269*	4:2	2056*		
8:4-6	2409*	6:1-6	2787*		
8:6	2449	6:2	627*	**Zephaniah**	
8:11	2835	6:6	589,* 2100*	2:3	64,* 711,* 716*
		11	219*	3:14	722,* 2676
Hosea		11:1-4	370*	3:17a	2676
1–3	1611*	11:1	219, 441,* 530*	3:17b	2676*

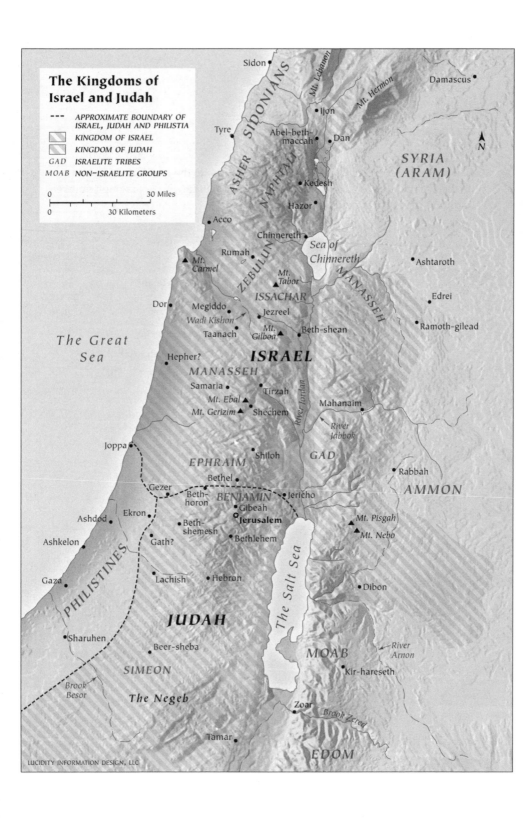

The Kingdoms of Israel and Judah

- - - APPROXIMATE BOUNDARY OF
ISRAEL, JUDAH AND PHILISTIA

KINGDOM OF ISRAEL

KINGDOM OF JUDAH

GAD   ISRAELITE TRIBES

MOAB   NON-ISRAELITE GROUPS

0   30 Miles

0   30 Kilometers

Sidon

Damascus

Mt. Lebanon

Ijon

Mt. Hermon

SIDONIANS

Tyre

Abel-beth-maccah

Dan

SYRIA
(ARAM)

N

ASHER

NAPHTALI

Kedesh

Acco

Hazor

Chinnereth

Sea of
Chinnereth

Ashtaroth

Rumah

ZEBULUN

Mt.
Carmel

Mt.
Tabor

MANASSEH

Edrei

ISSACHAR

Dor

Megiddo

Jezreel

Ramoth-gilead

Wadi Kishon

Mt.
Gilboa

Beth-shean

Taanach

The Great
Sea

ISRAEL

Hepher?

MANASSEH

Samaria

Tirzah

Mt. Ebal

Mahanaim

Mt. Gerizim

Shechem

River Jordan

River
Jabbok

Joppa

EPHRAIM

Shiloh

GAD

Bethel

Rabbah

Gezer

Beth-horon

BENJAMIN

Jericho

AMMON

Gibeah

Ashdod

Ekron

Jerusalem

Ashkelon

Beth-shemesh

Mt. Pisgah

Gath?

Bethlehem

Mt. Nebo

Gaza

PHILISTINES

Lachish

Hebron

The Salt Sea

Dibon

JUDAH

Sharuhen

Beer-sheba

MOAB

River
Arnon

SIMEON

Kir-hareseth

The Negeb

Brook
Besor

Zoar

Brook Zered

Tamar

EDOM

LUCIDITY INFORMATION DESIGN, LLC

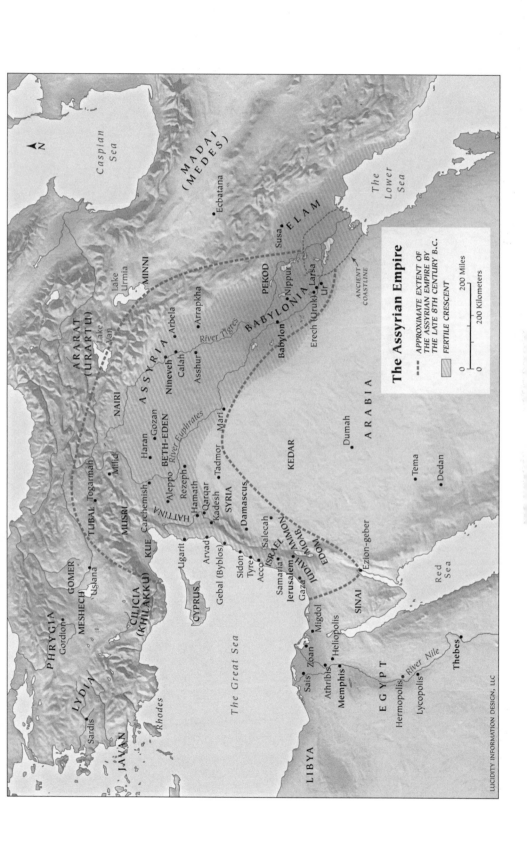

The Assyrian Empire

▪ ▪ ▪ APPROXIMATE EXTENT OF
THE ASSYRIAN EMPIRE BY
THE LATE 8TH CENTURY B.C.

FERTILE CRESCENT

0   200 Miles

0   200 Kilometers

Caspian Sea

MADAI
(MEDES)

Ecbatana

ELAM

Susa

The Lower Sea

MINNI

Lake Urmia

ARARAT
(URARTU)

Lake Van

Arbela

Arrapkha

Nineveh   PEKOD
Calah

Asshur   BABYLONIA   Nippur   Larsa
                           Erech (Uruk) Ur

Haran   Gozan   Babylon

NAIRI   BETH-EDEN

River Tigris

River Euphrates

ANCIENT
COASTLINE

ASSYRIA

Mitla

TUBAL Togarmah

MUSRI

GOMER

Tushana

MESHECH

PHRYGIA
Gordion

LYDIA

Sardis

JAVAN

Rhodes

CYPRUS

CILICIA
(KHILAKKU)

KUE   Carchemish

Aleppo

Rezeph   Mari

Hamath

Qarqar

Kadesh   Tadmor

SYRIA

Damascus

Ugarit

Arvad

Gebal (Byblos)

Sidon

Tyre

Acco   Salecah

Samaria   AMMON

Jerusalem   MOAB

Gaza   EDOM

JUDAH

ISRAEL

SINAI   Ezion-geber

The Great Sea

KEDAR

Dumah

ARABIA

Tema

Dedan

Red Sea

Migdol

Zoan

Sais   Athribis   Heliopolis

Memphis

Hermopolis

EGYPT

River Nile

Lycopolis

Thebes

LIBYA

LUCIDITY INFORMATION DESIGN, LLC

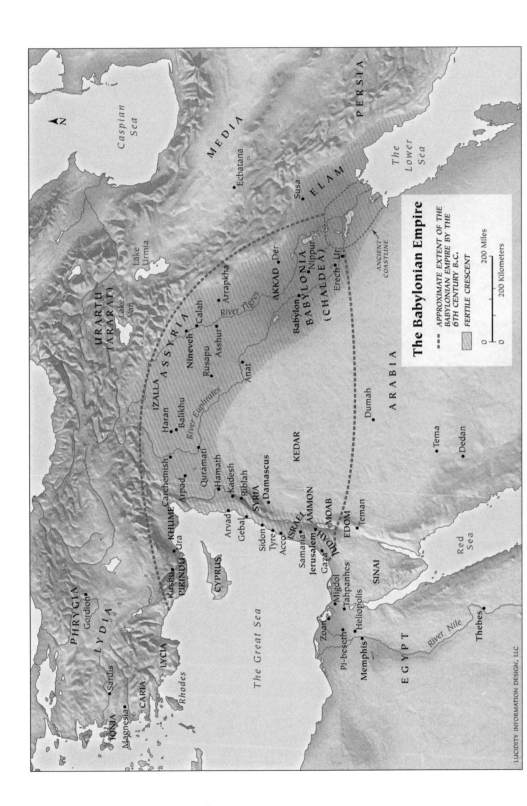

The Babylonian Empire

- - - APPROXIMATE EXTENT OF THE
BABYLONIAN EMPIRE BY THE
6TH CENTURY B.C.

FERTILE CRESCENT

0   200 Miles

0   200 Kilometers

N

*Caspian
Sea*

PHRYGIA

Gordion•

LYDIA

Sardis•

CARIA

LYCIA

IONIA

Magnesia•

Rhodes

The Great Sea

CYPRUS

URARTU
(ARARAT)

Lake
Van

Lake
Urmia

MEDIA

Ecbatana•

IZALA

ASSYRIA

Haran•

Balikhu•

Nineveh•

Calah•

Rusapu•

Asshur•

Arrapkha•

Der•

River Tigris

AKKAD

Susa•

ELAM

PERSIA

Carchemish•

Quramati•

Arpad•

Hamath•

Kadesh•

Riblah•

Damascus•

Anat•

River Euphrates

Babylon•

Nippur•
BABYLONIA
(CHALDEA)

Erech• Ur•

ANCIENT
COASTLINE

*The
Lower
Sea*

KHUME

Kirshu• Ura•

PIRINDU

Arvad•

Gebal•

Sidon•

Tyre•

Acco•

SYRIA

Samaria•

ISRAEL

Jerusalem•

AMMON

Gaza• JUDAH

MOAB

EDOM

Teman•

KEDAR

Dumah•

ARABIA

Tema•

Dedan•

SINAI

*Red
Sea*

Zoan•

Migdol•

Tahpanhes•

Pi-beseth•

Heliopolis•

Memphis•

EGYPT

River Nile

Thebes•

LUCIDITY INFORMATION DESIGN, LLC